D1563698

Ancient Peoples and Places

COLOMBIA

General Editor

DR. GLYN DANIEL

ABOUT THE AUTHOR

Gerardo Reichel-Dolmatoff, born in Austria, was educated in Vienna, Munich, and at the University of Paris. A resident of Colombia since 1939, he formed part of the group which, under the direction of the late Professor Paul Rivet, organized archaeological and ethnological research in that country. As a Government Anthropologist for more than twenty years, he has done extensive field work and has conducted excavations in many parts of the tropical lowlands. He has written several books on Colombian aboriginal cultures and has contributed numerous articles to specialised journals. He is now chairman of the Department of Anthropology at the University of los Andes, Bogota.

Ancient Peoples and Places

COLOMBIA

G. Reichel-Dolmatoff

65 PHOTOGRAPHS
66 LINE DRAWINGS
2 MAPS
2 TABLES

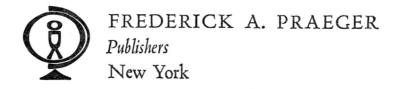

FREDERICK A. PRAEGER
Publishers
New York

THIS IS VOLUME FORTY-FOUR IN THE SERIES
Ancient Peoples and Places
GENERAL EDITOR: DR. GLYN DANIEL

BOOKS THAT MATTER

Published in the United States of America
In 1965 by Frederick A. Praeger, Inc.,
Publishers, 111 Fourth Avenue
New York 3, N.Y.
All rights reserved
© G. Reichel-Dolmatoff 1965
Library of Congress Catalog Card Number: 65–23078
Printed in The Netherlands
by Koninklijke Drukkerij G.J. Thieme N. V., Nijmegen

CONTENTS

ILLUSTRATIONS

8

9

TO ALICIA

Preface

THIS BOOK IS A TENTATIVE OUTLINE of prehistoric cultural developments in Colombia, the old Kingdom of New Granada of Spanish colonial times, the colourful country of El Dorado of myth and romance. For years I had it in my mind to write this book and when Dr Glyn Daniel and the publishers asked me to undertake the task I gladly accepted the opportunity. But now, with the finished manuscript lying before me and as I sit down to write the preface to the chapters that follow, I recognize its many shortcomings. Colombia is an extremely complex country and to present a coherent picture of any aspect, be it history, geography, or its characteristics as a modern nation, is a task few if any have accomplished successfully, or to the satisfaction of the reader. The first chapters of this book will make it clear how strongly the varied physical environment has influenced man's tenure of this land and how profoundly the country's past and present have been shaped by contacts with neighbouring areas. Even more difficult is it to try to reconstruct the prehistoric past, not only because of the lack of archaeological information, but also on account of the complex relationships implied by Colombia's topographical and climatic peculiarities and its position on the American continent.

In the following chapters I have tried to gather together the many isolated threads of archaeological evidence and to weave them into a fabric which shows a pattern, a set of regularities in time and space. In doing this I have had to refer often to my own field-work, but I have also drawn widely upon the work of others, not only in the discipline of archaeology, but also in the fields of geography, palaeontology, zoology, and botany. My debt to all these specialists is gratefully acknowledged.

I would also like to express my gratitude to Dr Sylvia Broad‑
bent of the Department of Anthropology, Universidad de los
Andes, for reading part of the manuscript and making many
helpful suggestions. My wife, herself a professional anthropol‑
ogist, has worked with me in the field and in the laboratory, and
her contribution to the writing of this book has been very sub‑
stantial. Dr Thomas van der Hammen, of the Geologisch en
Mineralogisch Instituut of the University of Leyden, has most
generously given of his time in discussing, reading, and revising
the sections on climatic changes in the past. I should especially
like to thank Mr Alec Bright, of the Universidad de los Andes,
for his great patience in revising and correcting the manuscript,
and to Mrs Pauline Bright for the excellent drawings which
accompany the text. The maps were drawn by Mr H.A.Shel‑
ley, of Cambridge. I am also indebted to many institutions and
friends who helped me obtain the illustrations, and special
thanks are due to Dr Manuel J.Casas Manrique, Director of
the Instituto Colombiano de Antropología, Dr Luis Barriga
del Diestro of the Museo del Oro, and Mr Abdu Eljaiek who
took many of the photographs. To Dr Glyn Daniel I am most
grateful for his having asked me to write this book, and to the
staff of Thames and Hudson for their unfailing help and guid‑
ance in producing it.

G. R. ‑ D.

CHAPTER I

Introduction

THE STUDY OF COLOMBIAN PREHISTORY is still in its very initial stages. Overshadowed by the splendour of the ancient civilizations of Mexico-Guatemala and Peru-Bolivia, or 'Mesoamerica' and the 'Central Andes', to use the archaeologist's terminology, the prehistoric cultures of most other Latin American countries have never exercised the same attraction, nor caused the same awe and admiration as one feels when walking through the halls of Mexico's great museums or when standing before the temples of Tikal, or the mountain city of Machu Picchu. Great empires, large cities or temples never existed in the 'Intermediate Area', i.e. in Central America, Colombia, and Ecuador, nor were there any forts or irrigation works to speak of, nor stately tombs of warriors or priests. There were only small chiefdoms, or at most incipient states, scattered over the mountain flanks or on the coasts, leaving behind no great monuments but only the all too sparse remains of a simple way of life – the life of forest dwellers or highland farmers, of fishermen and villagers. And so the great museum expeditions from Europe or North America took little or no interest in these countries. With few exceptions they went to the heart-land of the great aboriginal civilizations. The local governments themselves were not much concerned about their own prehistoric antiquities – about sherds and stones left behind by 'savage' peoples long forgotten.

It is only in the last few decades that archaeologists have come to appreciate the importance of this Intermediate Area, of the Northern Andes, the region of the Isthmus, and the jungle-covered coastal plains. American prehistory – if it was to be a a comparative study – did not make sense if it did not take into account the ancient peoples of these regions. True, they had never reached the same level of development as the Mesoamerican and Central Andean civilizations, but the local achievements of the Intermediate Area should not be underestimated nor should their role be ignored as intermediaries and transmitters of cultural stimuli coming from many sides and at different periods. Aboriginal gold-work in the Americas reached its highest development in Colombia. Since ancient times Colombia's mountain valleys, with their innumerable microclimates, have been an ideal laboratory for plant domestication. The Colombian coasts and inter-Andean valleys must have been important migration and trade routes linking together vast areas lying to the north, south, and east. In many respects Colombia occupied a key position, midway between the two great cultural foci of the north and south, and as such became of increasing importance for all studies concerned with the wider interrelationships of American Indian cultures. Today, these, and many other theoretical aspects of Colombia's role in American prehistory are becoming increasingly recognized, making the study of this country's archaeological past one of the most interesting and promising fields in the New World.

Before turning to the difficult task of trying to offer, in the following pages, a more or less coherent picture of prehistoric cultural developments in Colombia, it is necessary to present first a short outline of the history of archaeological discovery and research in this country.[1]

Colombia is the land of El Dorado, the 'Gilded Man' – of emeralds and buried treasure, of gold at hand in mountains and lakes, and golden hoards hidden away in tombs. Gold and pearls were the first objects the Spanish explorers found among the Indians of the Caribbean coast, and gold soon became their obsession. They took it from the living and from the dead, by torture and violence, and by looting shrines and graves. The search for gold soon became a decisive factor in determining the routes of the conquering troops and in the choice of sites for the establishment of the first Spanish settlements. No wonder the friars and captains who became the first chroniclers of these exploits, when writing of the treasures found or hoped for, make much of these precious objects or the tombs opened and plundered by the soldiers. The chronicles speak of golden 'eagles' and crowns, breast-plates and diadems, nose rings and bracelets; found, stolen, received as gifts, traded for glass beads, extorted as tributes, or looted from the tombs of chieftains, to be melted into ingots and sent to Spain. As early as 1530, the governor of Santa Marta, García de Lerma, decreed that ancient burial places of the Tairona tribe could be opened only with his personal permission, in order to establish the rights of the Spanish Crown over the gold found in them. In 1572, a royal decree demanded that half the gold found in the rich burial mounds of the Sinú region should be delivered to the Crown, and similar rules were applied by most local authorities to control the digging and looting, and to guarantee that the Spanish treasury received its share.

But little else is said in the chronicles of the conquest, about monuments or constructions belonging to the Indian past. There are a few remarks on the stone buildings of the Tairona, on the burial mounds of the Sinú, on some irrigation channels here and there, but otherwise these remains of the past did not interest the Spaniards. The idols and shrines were easily destroyed, most of them being of wood, and as the conquerors found no large ruins or monuments comparable to those their contemporaries were discovering in Mexico and Peru, the chroniclers give no descriptions of what to them seemed of no importance. The culture of some of the Indian tribes they do, however, describe in some detail and here we find valuable information on settlement patterns and agricultural techniques, on religion and magic, burial rites and warfare, weapons and tools, and a great many other aspects which can help the archaeologist to interpret some of the ancient remains he is discovering today. There exist

some fairly extensive accounts of Chibcha culture, of the Tairona and Quimbaya Indians, and of a number of other chiefdoms or small tribal groups. The chroniclers of the sixteenth
and seventeenth centuries are therefore sources of importance and
much information of value can be gleaned from these early
documents.[2]

The accounts of eighteenth-century historians and travellers
contain only sparse information. In 1757, Juan de Santa Gertrudis, a Spanish friar, visited the head-waters of the Magdalena
river and wrote a naive but interesting account of the monolithic statues of San Agustín, a manuscript which for two hundred years remained unpublished; and forty years later, in 1797,
the Colombian naturalist Francisco José de Caldas visited the
same region and mentions the famous archaeological site in a
later publication (1808). Alexander von Humboldt was the
first traveller to write on the ancient petroglyphs and pictographs
of the Orinoco region. In his account of explorations undertaken in 1801 in the interior provinces of Colombia, he de-
scribes the sacred lake of Guatavita near Bogotá, where the
Chibcha chieftains made their traditional offerings of gold, and
writes in some detail of the theories of Father José Domingo
Duquesne, a parish priest from the Bogotá highlands who mis-
took a small relief-carved stone used for embossing gold, for a
Chibcha calendar. From then on, and certainly under the stim-
ulus of Humboldt's influential books, the prehistoric cultures of
Colombia, above all of the Chibcha, are mentioned more frequently by other travellers and *savants*. For curiosity's sake one
may mention here M. de Paravey's *Mémoire sur l'origine japonaise,
arabe et basque de la civilisation des peuples du plateau de Bogotá,* published in Paris in 1835, which shows the rather fantastic trend
some of the speculations on the origins of the American Indian
were taking at that time.

About the middle of the last century, we meet the first Colombian antiquarians and pioneers of archaeological research.

In 1848, Joaquín Acosta published his *Compendio histórico del descubrimiento y colonización de la Nueva Granada* in Paris, and included some illustrations of Chibcha and Tairona artifacts; Ezequiel Uricoechea wrote his *Memoria sobre las antigüedades neogranadinas* (Berlin, 1854). Among foreign scholars we have Rivero and Tschudi's *Antigüedades Peruanas* (including some from Colombia) published in Vienna in 1851, and William Bollaert's *Antiquarian, Ethnological, and Other Researches in New Granada, Equador, Peru and Chile* (London, 1860). By the end of the century, the Colombian historian Liborio Zerda had written *El Dorado: Estudio histórico, etnográfico y arqueológico de los Chibchas* (Bogotá, 1883); Manuel Uribe Angel had published his *Geografía general y compendio histórico del Estado de Antioquia*, with 34 engraved plates illustrating archaeological objects from western Colombia (Paris, 1885); and Carlos Cuervo Márquez had written *Prehistoria y Viajes,* describing sites in the San Agustín, Tierradentro, and Santa Marta regions (Bogotá, 1893). In 1895, Vicente Restrepo published his *Atlas Arqueológico,* with 46 large plates, as a supplement to his still classic work, *Los Chibchas antes de la conquista española.* We cannot enumerate here all the authors, both Colombian and foreign, who took an interest in the prehistoric remains of the country before the turn of the century. They were historians, antiquaries, or occasional travellers who described what they saw or heard, and often enough incorporated into their writings the speculations their predecessors had made about the origins and meaning of these ancient remains. Father Duquesne's spurious 'calendar stone', for example, has haunted the literature for almost a century and a half.

It was not until 1913 that the first systematic excavations were carried out in Colombian territory. From 1913 to 1914, Konrad Theodor Preuss, of the Museum für Völkerkunde, Berlin, worked at San Agustín, and in 1929 his great work *Monumentale vorgeschichtliche Kunst,* containing the first detailed excavation report on a Colombian prehistoric culture, was published in

Göttingen. The next major excavations were carried out by J. Alden Mason who, in 1922–23, worked in the Tairona area of the Sierra Nevada of Santa Marta, on behalf of the Field Museum of Natural History (now the Chicago Natural History Museum). Mason's three-volume report, published between 1931 and 1939, was a milestone in archaeological research, calling attention to a region hitherto unexplored. Sigvald Linné's work in the Darien area (1929) added important knowledge on the region of the Isthmus. In the following years we find a number of other foreign archaeologists working in various parts of Colombia: Gustaf Bolinder (1937; 1942) in the Bogotá highlands and the Tairona area; Henry S. Wassén (1937) in the Western Cordillera, and Gregory Mason (1940), also in the Tairona area.

In 1935, the Colombian government established an 'Archaeological Park' at San Agustín – the now famous site where in the early thirties the Italian Federico Lunardi (1934; 1935) and the Belgian Robert de Wavrin (1932) had been working. From 1936 to 1937, the first archaeological expedition sponsored by the Ministry of National Education worked at San Agustín, under the direction of the Spanish archaeologist José Pérez de Barradas, having as his assistant Gregorio Hernández de Alba, a young Colombian archaeologist who, with his enthusiasm and energy, soon became a leading influence. In 1938, thanks mainly to the efforts of Hernández de Alba, the Ministry of National Education established the Archaeological Service (Servicio Arqueológico), an institution which began to arrange exhibits, carried out research, and organized the protection of prehistoric monuments. The archaeological section of the old National Museum was completely remodelled, and, enriched by recent finds and acquisitions, an important exhibition was opened the same year to celebrate the fourth centenary of the founding of Bogotá by the Spanish conqueror Gonzalo Jimenez de Quesada.[3]

In 1939, Colombia's semi-official Banco de la República took a momentous decision. Over the years, as a matter of fact ever since the Spanish conquest, treasure-hunters and grave-looters had traded with the prehistoric gold objects found in their illegal, but hardly preventable, excavations in the remoter areas. Now the governing body of the bank, with the backing of its manager Julio Caro, decided to buy from private collectors or from occasional discoverers – the latter mostly peasants or *guaqueros* (professional grave-robbers) – those artifacts which otherwise would be scattered and melted down, assembling and preserving in this way an unequalled treasure of ancient Indian gold. The bank, which considers its Gold Museum not as a form of capital investment but as a true cultural enterprise, now has a fabulous collection of over 8,000 objects manufactured by the aboriginal goldsmiths, who were the most skilful in ancient America.

The year 1941 marked another turning-point in archaeological research: the arrival in Bogotá of the famous director of the Musée de l'Homme of Paris, Paul Rivet. He spent the war years in Colombia, gathering around him a group of students and founding an official centre for training and research, the Instituto Etnológico Nacional. Rivet's teachings and writings have had a lasting influence upon all fields of anthropological work in Colombia. Systematic field research was organized under his direction, journals were founded to publish their results, and a group of students underwent training in archaeology, ethnology, linguistics, and physical anthropology. By 1945, the Institute had absorbed the Archaeological Service, and in 1952, the name of the institution was officially changed to Instituto Colombiano de Antropología, as a branch of the Ministry of Education and with offices in the new National Museum. It is this group which has contributed most effectively to a better knowledge of the country's prehistory, and which has carried on the tradition established by Paul Rivet. Julio

César Cubillos, Luis Duque Gómez, Eliécer Silva Celis, to name only a few, were among the first Colombian archaeologists who began to make systematic surveys and publish detailed excavation reports.

During 1941–42, the Yale Archaeological Expedition, under Wendell C. Bennett and James A. Ford, dug in the Cauca valley and made a survey of museum and private collections. In 1952–53 the German archaeologist H. Nachtigall worked in San Agustín and Tierradentro, and recently (1961, 1963), two archaeological expeditions from Cambridge, under Warwick Bray, have carried out work in the Calima and Cauca valleys. From 1960 to 1962, the Institute of Andean Research, of Washington, under the sponsorship of the National Science Foundation, developed a major research project on the Pacific coast between Mexico and Peru, and I and my wife were put in charge of the Colombian Pacific sector, while Carlos Angulo Valdés, of the Universidad del Atlántico, at Barranquilla, covered part of the Caribbean coast. Over the years, I have worked mainly in the Caribbean lowlands and the Sierra Nevada of Santa Marta, and my familiarity with these regions is, of course, reflected in the chapters that follow.

Although, as we have seen, considerable research has been carried out in the last fifty years, it is also obvious that most of it has concentrated on certain rather limited regions: San Agustín, Tierradentro, the Sierra Nevada of Santa Marta, the Chibcha territory around Bogotá, and the two coasts. This means that there still remain immense regions where hardly any archaeological work has been done: the Central Cordillera, the Magdalena and Cauca valleys, the Andean South, the highlands north of Bogotá and, of course, the vast lowlands lying to the east of the cordilleras, toward the Orinoco and Amazon basins. But even in those regions where excavations have been carried out over the years, concrete information on ceramic typologies and their local sequences is largely lacking and hardly any at-

Introduction

tempt has been made to correlate the different prehistoric cultures and to trace their development in space and time.

Some general divisions into 'archaeological areas', in a purely
spatial sense and without time-depth, have been postulated by
several authors whose publications are quoted in the bibliography.[4] The lack of absolute dates and of clearly defined strati-
graphic sequences has, until recently, made it almost impossible,
or, to say the least, highly dubious, to attempt a wider correlation and a chronological framework. During the last decade a
series of radiocarbon dates have become available for Colombia,
and these, together with a number of local sequences, are now
beginning to suggest a tentative picture of the time-depth and
cultural interrelationships of Colombia's prehistoric peoples. I
am well aware of the great difficulties involved in trying to trace
these developments, on the basis of the scanty evidence available
at present. For the purposes of this book I have endeavoured to
combine, whenever this was possible, an area approach with a
chronological one. Within this framework I have tried to trace
the major stages of development, from the first peopling of the
country, to the first contacts with the European discoverers. Any
such attempt to construct a general theory from the mass of dis-
ordered data, must necessarily be a provisional one and it is
quite probable that future research will prove some of the conclusions to be wrong.

A word must be said here about the character of archaeological field research in a country like Colombia, about the nature
of the evidence, and about the manner in which it is obtained
and interpreted. Field conditions are very different from those
encountered in Europe or the Near East, in North America or
on the Peruvian coast. In the Colombian rain-forests, the savannahs, or the steep mountain slopes of the Andes, there are few
surface features to guide the archaeologist in his search for prehistoric remains. Many sites have been disturbed, or totally destroyed, by the exuberant vegetation or by deep erosion and

landslides, by flooding and torrential rains, by roots, or by bur-
rowing animals. Others are hidden under deep river deposits or
in the jungle. Year after year the rivers and streams erode the
banks where ancient sites are located, and human agencies, agriculture, cattle, road-building or housing developments destroy
others. Once located, the sites themselves often provide only
most limited information. Architectural features in the form of
stone constructions or earthworks are very rare; road and field
systems are difficult to appraise because of their vegetation cover
or erosion; skeletal remains are preserved only under special
conditions such as prevail in dry caves. There are but few metal
objects, hardly ever tools. Few objects of bone are preserved and
such things as basketry, textiles, or wooden implements are
found only by lucky chance in a cave or an extremely dry burial
chamber. Even lithic artifacts are not very numerous or varied.

But there are potsherds, thousands upon thousands of them,
marking house sites and middens, camps or villages; small bits
of broken vessels made in different techniques, in different shapes,
bearing different kinds of decoration. These sherds, often
enough a drab lot but full of meaning in the hands of the specialist, are the true key to the reconstruction of the past. Lacking
the fuller record preserved in other lands and climates, the archaeologist must make the fullest use of these small fragments of
broken pots, tracing their developments, comparing them from
stratum to stratum and from site to site; interpreting from their
shapes their probable use; examining them for imprints of seeds,
basketry, textiles or netting, in short, probing them to the utmost of his logical capacity and ingenuity and, last but not least,
in the light of his ethnological knowledge of the modern tropical
and sub-tropical Indian tribes. On the other hand, fullest use
must be made of ecological data, of climatology, geomorpholo-
gy, faunistic remains and site location, in order to evaluate the
economic basis of the different prehistoric cultures. These two
aspects, then – pottery analysis and ecological considerations in

their widest sense – must be the guiding principles in our attempt at deciphering Colombia's past, and if, in the chapters
that follow, the reader finds again and again descriptions of
pottery types and tentative appraisals of ecological conditions in
the past, he must remember the limited evidence which forms
the sparse record left behind by these long-vanished peoples
whose daily life and slow cultural evolution we are trying to
reconstruct.

CHAPTER II
The Land

COLOMBIA IS LOCATED in the extreme north-western section of the South American continent where it occupies an area of almost 440,000 square miles, equalling in size the combined areas of France, Spain and Portugal. This immense land with its exuberant jungles and rugged mountains, stretching from the Caribbean to the Amazon, is South America's 'corner house'; alone among the countries in the southern hemisphere, Colombia has two coast lines: on the Atlantic and on the Pacific. While the south-eastern two-thirds of the country form part of the Amazon basin and the Orinoco plains, the mountainous interior constitutes the northernmost extension of the great Andean chain.

Fig. 1

Colombia's extreme diversity of land configuration, meteorological features, and cultural developments has always defied any attempt at clear-cut description. Few countries in the world equal its environmental variety. Owing both to its unique geographical location and to its particularly complex physiographical and climatological characteristics, the territory of the Republic of Colombia forms the real core-land of the Intermediate Area, that is to say the lands which lie between the two major centres of aboriginal American civilization. In the course of its native history, this country has played a most varied but always important role. Its general location and particular complexity have made of Colombia both a gateway and a bottleneck, a cross-roads and a *cul-de-sac,* a centre of convergence and of diffusion, a splendid biological laboratory and a mosaic of ecological niches, where the struggle between human adaptive resources and natural environmental forces has continued up to the present day. It would be difficult indeed to find elsewhere in the Americas a more varied landscape for man to cope with. All these factors tend, of course, toward extreme cultural diversity, and diversity will always be the keyword in any discussion of Colombia.[5]

The main structural feature of the country is the mountain ranges which divide the land into three main regions: the Andean region, the Eastern Plains, and the Coastal Lowlands. Upon entering Colombia, the Andes lose their former unity and divide into three huge mountain chains: the Western, Central, and Eastern Cordilleras, which fan out from the south and stretch across the country, from the Ecuadorian highlands to the flat Caribbean coast in the north. Approximately parallel to these continuous ranges, there lie the wide valleys of the Magdalena and Cauca rivers flanked by lofty mountain chains which, here and there, are crowned with snow peaks and towering volcanoes. These two rivers, the true life-lines of the country, flow into the Caribbean shortly after the Cauca has joined the Magdalena on the wide flood-plains of the north.

East of the Andes and beyond the cordilleras, there lie the immense peripheral areas of the Orinoco plains and the Amazon forests, constituting two-thirds of the nation's territory. These sparsely populated and remote regions have never played an important part in the cultural development of the country, whose heart-land has always been the slopes and valleys of the cordilleras together with the coasts and northern alluvial plains.

Lying between 12° 30′ north and 4° 13′ south of the Equator, most of the territory of Colombia has a tropical climate, but as temperature depends on altitude, the climatic range of the mountainous parts of the country covers the entire scale from humid or dry tropics to the cold Andean highlands and snow peaks. A fourfold division into major climatic levels shows this range: first, there is the *tierra caliente* or hot country, from sea level to about 1,000 m., which forms 83% of the national territory, with a mean annual temperature exceeding 24° C. The *tierra templada* (temperate country) follows between 1,000 and 2,000

m., covering some 9% of the territory and having a mean temperature of not less than 17.5° C. Between 2,000 and 3,000 m.,
there lies the so-called *tierra fría* or cold country, which covers
some 6% of the national territory and has a mean annual temperature nowhere less than 12° C.; and just above 3,000 m.,
there begins the *páramo,* the tundra-like barren highlands which
cover some 2% of the land and have a temperature below 12° C.
The lower limit of perpetual snow is at some 4,500 to 4,800 m.

In Colombia the seasons are marked by rainfall and not by
major fluctuations of temperature. On the Caribbean coastal
plain, north of latitude 8° N, there is a rainy season of about
eight months (April to November), followed by a dry season of
some four months (December to March), while to the south of
this latitude the rainy season is generally interrupted by a short
intermediate period of little rainfall in June and July. In the
Pacific lowlands there is hardly a dry season at all, the rains
lasting practically the whole year round. The annual distribution, frequency, and quantity of precipitation depend, of course,
on many local factors. While the Guajira Peninsula in the north
receives only about 200 mm. of annual rainfall, the Pacific coast
with as much as 10,000 mm. is probably the rainiest and most
humid area of the entire American tropics.

One might think, perhaps, that these are pedantic facts which
make dreary reading. But they become stark reality and acquire
significance when we ask ourselves: What did this country
mean to the first settlers? How did these people cope with their
environment? How did this landscape influence the first beginnings of village farming? Coast and peak, marshy plains and
barren highlands, the sluggish rivers meandering through the
rain-drenched forests, the quiet, sunlit beaches – how did they
contribute in shaping the cultures and societies which, millennia and centuries ago, called them their home?

In trying to answer these and many other questions, we must
look for smaller units of topography and climate, units which

Fig. 1.   *Principal topographical features of Colombia*

are more intelligible and integrated. According to meteorologi⁄
cal and morphological factors, one can distinguish five large
natural areas which, although containing within them many
sub⁄areas that show marked contrasts, present a more or less
coherent aspect. These five areas are:
The Caribbean Lowlands
The Pacific Lowlands
The Andean Core
The Orinoco Plains
The Amazon Rain⁄forest
The Caribbean Lowlands stretch for about 1,600 km., from
the Venezuelan border to Panama, from the sterile sun⁄baked
deserts of the Guajira Peninsula to the mountainous, perennially
verdant jungles of Darien. The Guajira Peninsula forms the
northernmost tip of the South American continent. During the
dry season the trade winds blow steadily over this flat and sandy
expanse and, as there are no barriers to condense their humidity,
the Guajira is a vast, hot desert covered only by low xerophilous
shrubs, cacti and bromeliads. Only during the months of Oc⁄
tober and November do any rains fall and then the yellow desert
is suddenly covered with various shades of green. But for the
rest of the year, the Guajira is Colombia's driest territory – a
barren stretch of land surrounded by a violent sea.

To the south⁄west, the coastal plain continues, gradually
changing from desert to semi⁄arid savannah, with rolling hills
covered sometimes with large groves of shrubby deciduous trees
until, on reaching the Magdalena river, there opens up a wide
marshy flood plain dotted with lagoons and oxbow lakes – an
ever⁄changing labyrinth of swamps and channels. To the west
of the Magdalena, savannah⁄covered open hills continue, but as
the drying trade winds diminish in force, the annual rainfall in⁄
creases. Two large and important rivers, both having their sour⁄
ces close together in the mountainous jungle to the south, cross
these rolling plains which today are Colombia's main cattle⁄

breeding country. The Sinú river flows in a northward direc'
tion to the Caribbean, while the San Jorge river flows toward
the north'east and joins the Magdalena just below the latter's
confluence with the Cauca.

From the savannahs and groves east of the lower Magdalena
river, there rises the Sierra Nevada of Santa Marta, an isolated
mountain mass which emerges abruptly from the tropical low'
lands between the delta of the mighty river and the northern'
most outliers of the Eastern Cordillera. This mountain massif,
approximately pyramidal in shape, is the outstanding physio'
graphical feature of the Caribbean coast. In the Sierra Nevada
climate and vegetation change not only according to altitude,
but also in relation to slope exposure; the south'eastern slopes
which lie under the trade winds are covered with grassy savan'
nahs and a scanty growth of shrubs, while small groves of forest
exist only along the streams or in mountain folds which are
protected from the winds. The northern and western slopes are
much less exposed to the trade winds and are covered to a
greater extent with true forest. Rising close to the sea'shore and
surrounded by alluvial plains, the geographical position of the
Sierra Nevada imposes a certain degree of biological and cul'
tural isolation upon life, a fact we shall refer to later when speak'
ing of the prehistory of this area.

Toward its western extremity, the coastal plain merges with
the rain'forests of the Gulf of Urabá and the Darien range.
Low, marshy flood'plains and a fringe of mangrove swamps,
interrupted here and there by dark cliffs and boulder'strewn
beaches form a picturesque but inhospitable landscape.

The Pacific Lowlands present an altogether different picture.
Dense, tangled rain'forests stretch for more than 1,300 km. of
the low coast from Panama to Ecuador, all along the western
limit of Colombia. Large rivers such as the San Juan, Atrato,
and Baudó cross this territory together with hundreds of minor
streams and rivulets. The northern quarter is a cliffed coast with

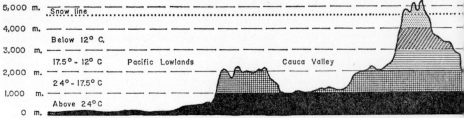

Fig. 2. Cross-section of the Colombian Cordilleras from the Pacific Coast to the Orinoco Plains

many deep inlets and natural harbours, but from Cape Corrientes southward, deep mangrove swamps and estuaries extend
along the coast in an ever-broadening belt which toward the
Ecuadorian border reaches a width of almost 8 km. With an
annual rainfall exceeding 7,000 mm. in its central part, the
Chocó, as the northern section of this territory is called, is one
of the true equatorial rain-forests of America. The dripping
hygrophilous vegetation cover, with its abundance of creepers
and epiphytic growth, is indeed a world apart from the dry
savannahs of the north coast or the rugged mountains of the
Andean interior.

Fig. 2

The Andean core-land has been mentioned already in its
major outline. The Central Cordillera is the highest, with an
average altitude of 3,000 m.; it is lower only toward its northern
end, where it divides into several ranges which finally dip into
the lowlands. The Eastern Cordillera has a mean altitude of
some 2,000 m. Being considerably broader than the others, it
forms several high plateaux, but it also divides into two ranges,
one of which continues toward the Caribbean and ends just
short of the Guajira Peninsula, while the other extends north-
eastwards and continues into Venezuela. The Western Cordillera is the lowest and shortest chain. But there are other mountains and mountain chains which do not form part of the Andean
system and which dot and streak the country in many places.
The Sierra Nevada of Santa Marta, Colombia's highest mountain range (5,775 m.), is structurally unrelated to the cordilleras.

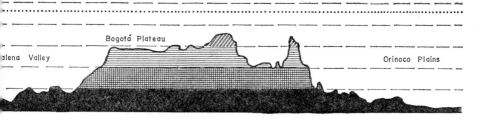

Bogotá Plateau

alena Valley

Orinoco Plains

Then there is the Serranía del Darien at the Panamanian border, which forms the continental watershed; the Serranía de la Ma-carena, just south of Bogotá, at the western rim of the Orinoco plains, which geologically belongs to the ancient Guiana Shield; and some minor ranges like the Serranía del Baudo and the Montañas de María, on the Pacific and Atlantic coasts respectively.

The three separate ranges of the cordilleras form an extremely irregular and complex relief of deep intermontane basins, savan-nah or forest-clad slopes, and cool upland regions with heavy forest or bleak desolate plateaux. The great variety of local con-ditions, such as altitude, slope exposure, prevailing air currents, humidity, the very nature of the soils, form here a mosaic of the most extreme complexity. The range of micro-environments within the wider ecological zones, each horizontally and verti-cally different in character, is certainly the most distinctive fea-ture of the Colombian cordilleras and their mountain-flanked valleys. A region of special importance is the *altiplano*, the high plateau approximately in the centre of the broad Cordillera Oriental. More than a dozen flat highland basins lie here at an elevation of some 2,700 m., forming with their fertile soils one of the most important areas of the country. The southermost basin forms the so-called Sabana de Bogotá, at an altitude of 2,600 m. above sea level. This is the centre of the district known as *Cundinamarca*, the 'Land of the Condor', the land of El Dorado.

It is obvious that the particular nature and scope of aborivginal cultural development in Colombia, from its earliest bevginnings to historical times, must be viewed and evaluated as a phenomenon which is intimately related to the unique physical and cultural position this country occupies in tropical Amervica. The prehistoric cultures of Colombia must always be seen against this background of extreme topographical and climatic diversity which, of course, have influenced and shaped many important aspects of the character and growth of the aboriginal societies. But what is more, Colombia is, and has always been, the gateway to South America, located at one of the major crossvroads of cultural exchange. Diffusion and stimuli reached Covlombia from north and south and spread – at different rates and at different times – from there to other regions, leading to a wide variety of local cultural developments in the intervAndean valvleys and coastal plains.

This leads us to the question of major natural migration routes and contact areas. The wide plain of the Caribbean Lowlands has undoubtedly been for thousands of years a region through which people moved back and forth, from the rivers to the interfluvial forests or from the seavshore to the fringes of the mountain ranges. The abundance, character, and timevdepth of the local archaeological record indicate this quite clearvly. The northernmost extension of the Eastern Cordillera was certainly not a barrier to these movements; it could be crossed at several convenient mountain passes towards what is now Venezuela. The Maracaibo basin, to the east, could also be reached by crossing the lower part of the Guajira Peninsula.

The Darien region in the northvwestern corner of Colombia where Central America joins the South American continent is, of course, a crucial contact area through which all early migravtions must have taken place, at least until the time when aborigivnal coastal navigation was sufficiently developed. The forbidvding aspect of the rainvforest which at present covers this region has led many people to believe that the narrow south-eastern portion of the Isthmus of Panama must have been a permanent obstacle to migration and direct diffusion between the Americas, but it is evident that small bands of migrating hunters and gatherers would have had no difficulty in crossing back and forth over the jungle-clad mountain folds or along the coasts. The impenetrable nature of the Darien has been greatly exaggerated, it seems, and if one takes into account the probability of changes in climate and vegetation in times past, during which the jungle was less dense, it is quite conceivable that even major migrations might have moved with relative ease from one part of the continent to another. Once in the Urabá region and on the lower Atrato river, migration toward the east finds hardly any obstacles at all. From the Guajira Peninsula it is easy to reach the Venezuelan north coast, and even the northernmost outliers of the Andes have a number of depressions offering contact with the lowlands beyond the mountain ranges.

The Pacific coast, which has probably experienced no considerable climatic changes, is certainly not a natural migration route as far as overland travel is concerned. On the contrary, the local conditions impede travel along the coast where deep mangrove swamps, cliffs, and innumerable rivers make it almost impossible to penetrate the land in a north-to-south direction, except further inland where the San Juan and Atrato rivers offer their waterways. However, from the coast toward the east there are several regions where a crossing over the mountains into the Cauca valley is fairly easy. The entire Western Cordillera, except for some spots, is rather low and by following some of the rivers, especially in the areas of the lower San Juan-Calima drainage or the Patía drainage, the inter-Andean valleys can be reached with ease.

The wide valleys of the Magdalena and Cauca are, of course, natural migration routes which have always played an important part in the movements of peoples and cultures. From the upper reaches of the Magdalena, the Eastern Cordillera can be crossed at several points. Beyond, the Orinoco plains and the Amazon basin open-up with their countless rivers running east and leading the way to the lowlands of Peru, Brazil, and the Guianas.

A word must be said here about the possibilities of aboriginal coastal navigation. The modern observer of a map of Colombia is often not aware of the fact that it is possible to travel by canoe from the Bay of Buenaventura to Ecuador without ever entering the sea (except for a very short passage across the Golfo de Tor-tugas), simply by using the network of estuaries and channels in the deep mangrove swamps at high tide. The same can be done when travelling north, from the San Juan delta to the mouth of the Baudó river. Only north of the Baudó does it become neces-sary to leave the protection of the mangrove swamps and to go out to the open sea, but during several months of the year, mainly from January to early April, the ocean is calm enough to make dug-out navigation possible. There are a few danger spots – Cape Corrientes, Cape Marzo, and some others – but even today the primitive Chocó Indians travel occasionally in their dug-outs from beach to beach. Balsa logs tied alongside the ca-noes provide a common means of stabilizing them. To a primi-tive people with any sea-faring knowledge at all this coast pre-sents few hazards and coastal navigation may well have been a major factor in early migrations, trade, and far-flung cultural diffusion. The same can be said of the Caribbean coast where, although there are hardly any mangrove swamps, it is possible to navigate from bay to bay during fair weather.

There exist then ample migration routes and possibilities of contact between major geographic and cultural areas: Central America, the coast of Ecuador, north-western Venezuela, the Orinoco plains, and the Amazon basin. These facts must be kept in mind as we now begin to trace the origins and devel-opments of aboriginal culture in this part of the continent.

Fig. 3

Fig. 3. Principal archaeological areas and sites

Key to Areas

1 Ranchería
2 Tairona
3 Lower Magdalena
4 Sinú
5 Chocó
6 Chibcha

7 Calima
8 Quimbaya
9 Tierradentro
10 San Agustín
11 Tumaco
12 Nariño

Sites: PUEBLITO

CHAPTER III

The Early Hunters and Gatherers

COLOMBIA'S MOUNTAINS, valleys and shore lines bear the eloquent marks of profound meteorological and topo-graphical changes which took place during the millennia of the Wisconsin Glacial Stage when the cyclic advance and re-treat of large ice masses in the northern latitudes shaped the face of the land and eventually set the stage for man's entrance into the Western Hemisphere. The submerged or raised coast lines, the coastal terraces which indicate oscillations in sea level, the many old river terraces which today lie high above the valley floors, the old lake beds and bogs in the Andean highlands, and the many traces of glacial action around the snow peaks of the cordilleras, give ample evidence of the profound changes the landscape underwent during Pleistocene times. Clearly these climatic fluctuations, with their consequent changes in fauna and flora, have had a far-reaching effect upon the Paleo-Indian's migrations and resources, and indeed upon his entire way of life.

Although most archaeologists will agree that America's first settlers arrived in small bands by way of the Bering Strait, dur-ing the Late Pleistocene, the crucial questions as to when this actually happened and what kind of culture they brought with them, is still being argued. While some believe that the first migrations from Asia arrived during, or shortly after, the Man-kato-Valders Advance (about 11,000 years ago) and were composed of specialized hunters in pursuit of large game, others favour the theory of much earlier migrations by groups of simple food-gatherers, unspecialized in their tools and ecological adap-tation. Our present state of knowledge leaves many aspects of the problem unclarified, as much depends on the interpretation given to certain lithic assemblages, on the precision of absolute dating techniques, and on the validity of faunistic or geological associations. But we do know for certain that man was present in South America some 10,000 years ago, and that he had reached by that time the southernmost tip of the continent. A look at the map will show us that there can be no doubt at all that Colombia was the first country in South America on which these early hunters and gatherers set foot on their long migration toward the south.

The Pleistocene and Holocene chronology of Colombia is still insufficiently known and hardly any studies of river terraces or glaciology have been carried out, nor have the biogeographic conditions which prevailed during prehistoric times been established in any detail. However, during recent years, some advances have been made in the study of lake and bog deposits, the pollen contents of which have been analyzed. As a matter of fact, modern studies of pollen diagrams from Colombia, especially from late Pleistocene and Holocene lake deposits in the highlands of the Eastern Cordillera, have provided some evidence for correlating the glacial and post-glacial successions not only of the two American continents but also of the Old and New Worlds. From these examinations based on pollen-analysis of the sequence of dominant tree and herb genera, it appears that the climatic phases of late-glacial and Holocene times in Colombia were approximately contemporary with the Old World phases and that the European succession of Boreal-Atlantic-Sub-Boreal-Sub-Atlantic periods is paralleled in Colombia by an identical succession of dry-wet-dry-wet periods, as can be inferred from the distribution of the weather-sensitive highland flora.

Fig. 4

The palynological studies carried out by Van der Hammen and González show a series of fluctuations both in the Andean tree line and in rainfall. During the cold periods of the Pleistocene, the tree line was some 1,200 m. lower than it is now, with a corresponding lowering of the temperature by 8° to 9° C, while at the time of the climatic optimum of the Holocene it was some 400 m. higher than at present. The correspondence of cold-to-wet, and warm-to-dry phases shows that, in the Colombian equatorial Andes, a glacial had also the characteristics of a plu-vial, and an inter-glacial also those of an inter-pluvial. The palynologists suggest that even the minor climate fluctuations in the Holocene of the Colombian cordilleras correspond in time with those of Europe.[6]

These observations throw an important light upon the prob-lem of man's entry into Colombia. At the time of the Indians' first appearance in South America, the only possible migration route, from Central America to the north-western corner of the southern continent, was the overland passage through the Isth-mus of Panama. The necessary navigational skill for sea-going craft to travel along the coast was developed only in more recent times, perhaps not more than 3,000 or 4,000 years ago, and all earlier contacts between the two continents, therefore, must have used the narrow pathway of the Darien. Nowadays, as we have already mentioned, this jungle-covered wilderness is considered by many to be an almost impassable obstacle to human migra-tions and its rain-forests, swamps, and dense underbrush are thought to form an impenetrable barrier. There is a plentiful literature describing this 'Green Hell', and the vicissitudes of travel in this region. In view of these extreme physical condi-tions, it is often held that only a small trickle of migrating In-dians could have reached South America, and that the Darien is, and has always been, a major obstacle to human migrations.

There is, of course, some truth in this, but there are also other considerations to be taken into account. In the first place, it is obvious that climatic changes during Late Pleistocene times would have influenced the Darien landscape and that during drier periods the jungle growth would have largely disappeared and a route would have presented itself. A drop in sea level, when much of the oceans' water was locked up in the continen-

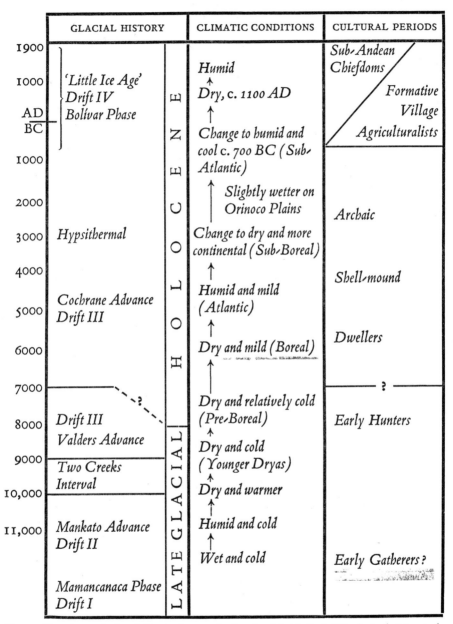

	GLACIAL HISTORY		CLIMATIC CONDITIONS	CULTURAL PERIODS
1900				*Sub-Andean*
			Humid	*Chiefdoms*
1000	*'Little Ice Age'*		*Dry, c. 1100 AD*	*Formative*
AD	*Drift IV*	H O L O C E N E		*Village*
BC	*Bolívar Phase*		*Change to humid and*	*Agriculturalists*
1000			*cool c. 700 BC (Sub-Atlantic)*	
2000			*Slightly wetter on Orinoco Plains*	*Archaic*
3000	*Hypsithermal*		*Change to dry and more continental (Sub-Boreal)*	
4000			*Humid and mild (Atlantic)*	*Shell-mound*
5000	*Cochrane Advance Drift III*			
6000			*Dry and mild (Boreal)*	*Dwellers*
7000				?
8000	*Drift III*	L A T E G L A C I A L	*Dry and relatively cold (Pre-Boreal)*	*Early Hunters*
	Valders Advance		*Dry and cold (Younger Dryas)*	
9000	*Two Creeks*			
10,000	*Interval*		*Dry and warmer*	
11,000	*Mankato Advance Drift II*		*Humid and cold*	
			Wet and cold	*Early Gatherers?*
	Mamancanaca Phase Drift I			

Fig. 4. Tentative correlation of climatic changes and cultural periods. Drifts I–IV refer to glaciations in the Sierra Nevada de Cocuy (Eastern Cordillera). The Bolívar and Mamancanaca phases are glaciations in the Sierra Nevada of Santa Marta

tal ice sheets, would have formed a land bridge about 160 km. wide. It has also been pointed out that a minor equatorward shift of the high-pressure belt of the Atlantic horse latitudes would lead to a southward and westward shift of the savannah climate and that a southward shift of 2° of the present border of savannah climate in northern Colombia would clear the route to South America. That the physical conditions of the Darien landscape have changed even since historical times can be seen from the accounts of the Spanish chroniclers of the sixteenth century who found, in what is today rain-forest and dense jun-gle, the open fields and large settlements of agricultural tribes.⁷

In the second place, even if tropical rain-forest conditions had prevailed during most of the time when the early southern mi-grations took place, the penetration of the Darien by successive bands of hunters and gatherers would have been a fairly easy matter. For those who have been born and raised in the forest, the Darien is no worse than many other rain-forest regions of the tropics through which we know that major migrations have been accomplished. There is a dry season from January to March, when the rains diminish greatly. At low tide one can walk for many kilometres along the sand beaches, and on the Pacific coast, between Panama and Colombia, there are no mangrove swamps at all. Small game, wild-growing fruits, fish, crabs, molluscs, and many other food resources are abundant in the Darien forest and are easily gathered by those who are familiar with the environment. We must never underestimate the endurance, the adaptability, and the inventiveness of the American Indian who often had to cope with the most adverse physical conditions on his migrations and on the long road to civilization.

Fig. 5   Although Colombia obviously was the first country of South America to be penetrated by the Paleo-Indian invaders from the north, archaeological knowledge of this early period is still very sparse. There is ample proof for the presence of early

44

	PACIFIC COAST	CAUCA VALLEY	ANDEAN MASSIF	MAGDALENA VALLEY	ATLANTIC COAST	EASTERN CORDILLERA	SIERRA NEVADA	LOWER GUAJIRA
1500								
1400	Minguimalo	Late Calima		Tamalameque Río de la Miel		Chibcha	Tairona	
1200	Cupica				Crespo	Los Santos	↑	↑
1000	Imbilí	↑	↑		↑			
800	Murillo							
600					Zambrano			
400					↑		Nahuanje	
200								Portacelli
AD	Mataje III							↑
BC	↑	'Quimbaya'			Momil II			Los Cocos
200	Mataje II Catanguero	↑		El Guamo	↑	Bochalema	Bonda	El Horno
400	Mataje I	Early Calima	San Agustín					↑ La Loma
600					Momil I			
800					Malambo			
1000					Barlovento			
1200					↑			
1400								
1600								
1800								
2000					Canapote			
2200					↑			
2400								
2600								
2800					Puerto Hormiga			
3000								

Fig. 5. Chronological table of principal cultures

Fig. 6. Projectile points from El Espinal, Ibagué, and Manizales

hunters from the neighbouring countries, from Venezuela and Ecuador; groups which necessarily must have crossed Colombian territory. But from Colombia itself no clear, datable evidence for these early peoples has come to light so far. Remains of Late Pleistocene mammals (mastodon, amerhippus, mylodon, eremotherium, etc.) have been found in several localities, but there is no proven association between these fossil bones and human artifacts, nor have there been any finds of human skeletal remains which could be attributed to an early time level. This dearth of information is probably not due to an extreme scarcity of sites, but reflects rather the lack of systematic research.

There exist, however, a few isolated finds which, although all of them come from eroded surface sites, can probably be attributed to a Paleo-Indian occupation. Two categories of finds can be distinguished here: chance finds of projectile points, and large assemblages of other lithic artifacts. One flint projectile point was found near El Espinal, in the Tolima district, in a layer of clay overlain by more than 7 m. of sand and volcanic ash. It is of lanceolate shape, with a short, broad stem produced by steep shouldering; the base is slightly concave. The object is

46

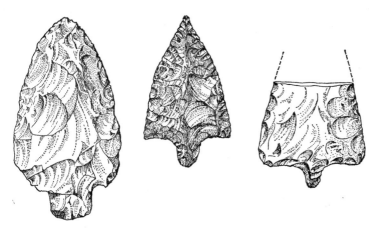

Fig. 7. Projectile points from Santa Marta, Mahates, and Betancí

bifacially flaked by controlled percussion and the slightly serrated edges show oblique-parallel pressure retouch. Similar *Fig. 6*
points have been found occasionally in other localities of the
Tolima district, most of them bearing a superficial resemblance
to the so-called Angostura points of North America. Typologically quite different is a projectile point found near Manizales,
in the Central Cordillera. This short, blunt, slightly shouldered point is provided with a long stem which ends in a bifurcate base; the bifacial percussion flaking is rather crude. There
are certain similarities with Pinto Basin points from California
and with some of the smaller specimens of the Patagonian sequence (Patagonia I). From the Caribbean coast come a number of small stemmed points, all percussion flaked except for *Fig. 7*
one delicately pressure-flaked point from Mahates. An
interesting point derives from the Western Cordillera: to the
bifacial percussion flaking there is added an irregular secondary *Fig. 8*
retouch along the edges. Two longitudinal flakes have been
removed from the slightly fish-tail-shaped stem, producing a
'fluted' effect. The point measures 9.1 cm. in length. These stray
finds, although suggestive, are, of course, difficult to place in

Fig. 8.
Projectile point
from Restrepo,
Western
Cordillera

time, but their general morphological and technological char-acteristics recall Paleo-Indian weapons found in other parts of the American continent.

The other category of possible Paleo-Indian remains is prob-ably of still greater significance. In recent years, several well-defined lithic assemblages have been discovered in different re-gions of the country, the most important ones being located on the coastal plains of the Caribbean, while others were found on the Pacific coast and also in the interior provinces. At San Ni-colás, an eroded hill-top on the lower Sinú river, a large number of chipped flint artifacts were discovered, among them several tools such as irregular flake scrapers, a 'turtleback' scraper, some amorphous flake knives, and many partially modified stones. A few large cores, with striking platforms and well-marked negative percussion bulbs, also belong to this complex. Waste materials, rejects, and blanks were also found. The total assem-blage contains only unifacially chipped artifacts shaped mainly by percussion and only in rare cases by irregular pressure flak-ing.[8] Similar assemblages have been found in the region of Pomares, on the Canal del Dique, a silted-up arm of the Mag-

Fig. 9.   Scraper from Pomares

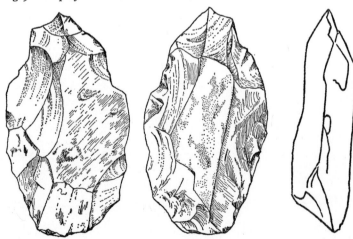

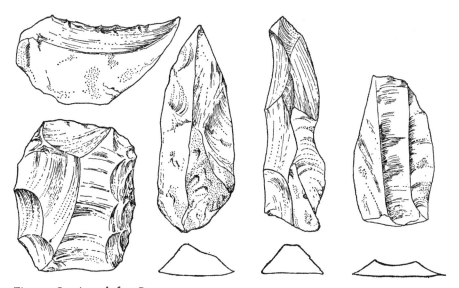

Fig. 10. Scraping tools from Pomares

dalena river. There, on the old river terraces, several hundred flint objects were found on the eroded surface. These assem-blages also consist mainly of scraping tools shaped by percus-sion flaking. On the Pacific coast, a large number of flint arti-facts were found on the upper Baudó, the Juruvidá, and the Chorí rivers, and on the inlet of Bahía de Utría. From the in-terior of Colombia there is the site of Bocas de Carare, at the mouth of the Carare river, with another lithic complex of a very similar nature.[9]

All these prehistoric stone industries have certain character-istics in common. All were found on eroded ridges or hill-tops, on old river terraces, or in gravel beds. Pottery associations, food-grinding implements, or any ground or polished stone artifacts, were absent. The total tool assemblages consisted main-ly of unifacial scrapers and knives, with a few chopping tools, a number of small boring or engraving tools, and no projectile points at all. Crude percussion flaking is predominant, with secondary retouch by controlled percussion or pressure flaking

49

occurring only rarely. The range of tools and the riverine or la-
goonal environment suggest bands of food gatherers and fishermen, but certainly not groups dependent upon hunting or cultivation. The emphasis upon scraping and cutting edges may well
be connected with the daily task of scaling and cleaning fish,
and with the manufacture of fishing gear or other wooden
instruments.

It is, again, very difficult to assign these lithic assemblages, or
the projectile points mentioned above, with any certainty to a
Paleo-Indian stage, but the very low technological level of the
scraping-tool complexes from the Atlantic and Pacific coasts,
as compared with later developments in and outside Colombia,
suggests an early period. Quite possibly, the lithic assemblages
mentioned here are representative of the so-called 'Pre-Projectile
Point' stage which might have preceded the Late Pleistocene
big-game hunters by many thousands of years.[10] But until these
artifacts have been found in controlled excavations and been
dated by reliable methods, no definite statement can be made as
to their age and wider cultural context.

There are many promising regions in Colombia where future
research might concentrate. The river terraces of the upper Magdalena valley, the surroundings of old Pleistocene lakes, the
obsidian deposits of the Central Cordillera, the caves of the
highlands north of Bogotá, and many other regions, are likely
spots where remains of the oldest inhabitants may eventually be
found. Systematic field surveys in these areas are urgently needed
if we want to know more about the most ancient settlers of
Colombia.

CHAPTER IV

The Shell-mound Dwellers

A TREND TOWARDS A MILDER CLIMATE, setting in about 7000 BC, caused an environmental shift affecting all aspects of ecology, and with them man's cultural adaptation to a slowly changing world. The large mammals were now dis-appearing, partly perhaps because their forage was becoming scarcer as a result of prolonged droughts and partly because man's specialized hunting techniques were leading to the ex-tinction of many species which until then had been his main food supply. Although it is possible that some species of Late Pleistocene fauna survived here and there in Colombia, in iso-lated niches, for longer periods than in North America, where desiccation was progressing faster, the general extinction of the large mammalian fauna was rather abrupt and accelerated the processes which led to new forms of adaptation for the roaming bands of big-game hunters. We know nothing at present of the cultural chronology of these events in Colombia, but it is evi-dent that the three or four thousand years at the beginning of the Holocene were a crucial period, when man had to develop new resources for survival which, eventually, came to form the foundations for settled life and food production.

About 3000 BC, there appears on the Caribbean seaboard of Colombia a well-defined pattern of life: the shell-mound dwel-lers. For the next 2,000 or more years, these peoples, much like their European counterparts, spread over the sea-shores and la-goons and established the way of life characteristic of the so-called Archaic or Pre-Formative Stage in the Americas. The stage of cultural development thus designated, like any other culture stage, is not strictly confined in time and space, but forms a long period of transition, from the Paleo-Indian hunting pattern in a Late Pleistocene environment, to a pattern of small-game hunt-

ing, fishing, and foraging, under climatic conditions quite similar to the present. The over-all time-span of this stage covers
perhaps some 6,000 years, roughly from 7000 to the first millennium BC, and it was during this period that the 'Meso-
Indians', as differentiated from their Paleo-Indian predecessors
and ancestors, struggled for a successful adjustment to new environmental conditions. The Meso-Indians were nomadic or
semi-nomadic gatherers who, often in seasonal cycles, established their camp-sites on sea-shores, rivers, estuaries, or swamps,
achieving eventually a very thorough and efficient exploitation
of their respective micro-environments by utilizing most or all
of the edible resources. In Colombia, this developmental stage is
represented by large accumulations of sea-shells which, among
other food resources, seem to have been the main protein source
of the small groups which lived next to, or often on top of,
these slowly growing mounds built up of empty, discarded
shells. We must describe the environmental and cultural characteristics of this stage in more detail because it was at this time
that these primitive peoples developed some of the specific traits
and abilities which, in later periods, provided the basis for a
more sedentary form of life.

The wide, hot alluvial plain bordering the Caribbean coast
and crossed by sluggish, meandering rivers, with their intricate
and ever-changing patterns of oxbow lakes and channels, became for many centuries – indeed, for millennia – the scene of a
slowly evolving culture-pattern which, step by step, grew into a
coherent unit. To groups of hunters, gatherers, and fisher-folk,
this land offered many advantages; there was the sea with its
abundant resources of fish and molluscs; the rivers, estuaries and
lagoons with their jungle and reed-covered margins where there
was plenty of large and small game, from waterfowl and turtles
to deer and peccary. There were crocodiles and caymans,
iguanas and other large lizards, rodents, monkeys, edible crabs
and clams, many wild-growing fruits – a land of plenty. Some

five thousand years ago, the climate of the northern part of Colombia was probably somewhat drier than it is today, but it was
beginning to become more humid at that time and continued
to do so until well after the start of our era, so that during the
two or three millennia preceding this date, what is today the
interfluvial savannah country was probably covered with luxuri-
ant jungle. At all events, it is here that the archaeological record shows clear-cut sequences and more time-depth than in
other regions of Colombia. This must have been a privileged
area, attractive to those simple peoples who used to roam and to
gather their food, long before a more settled way of life had
become possible.

The shell-fishing stations, established around 3000 BC at
several spots along the Caribbean coast, form the earliest known
and dated archaeological horizon in Colombia, and extensive
excavations in them have revealed a fairly detailed record of life
during the second and third millennia BC. The principal site
and the one which has yielded so far the oldest radiocarbon
dates is the Puerto Hormiga shell-mound, near the mouth of the
Canal del Dique.[11] This canal, constructed by the Spaniards
in the middle of the seventeenth century by linking together a
chain of shallow lagoons stretching between the lower Magdalena river and the coast south of Cartagena, makes use of a long
depression which formerly was a main outlet of the river. In due
course the canal silted up, changing into a chain of freshwater
lagoons and swamp-lands, whilst the river turned north to its
present outlet, but the conformation of the land still shows the
direction its ancient course had taken. At the time when the
Meso-Indians established themselves in this region, the river
was probably still flowing through this depression and the natural environment of their camp-sites thus offered them both
river resources and those provided by the neighbouring sea-shore.
The Puerto Hormiga site is located on low ground, only a few
metres above present sea level and, like other sites of this type,

consists of a low, ring-shaped accumulation of sea-shells, some 80 m. in diameter. The whole mound is formed by several super-imposed deposits of shell mixed with a variety of cultural remains, stone artifacts, and animal bones. At several periods of its occupation, parts of the mound had been levelled by its an-cient inhabitants, to be used as living platforms or floors, and the existence of hearths and layers of trampled shell clearly in-dicate that the mound was occupied, at different times, by groups of people who used it as a camp-site. The structure of the mound indicates that, from its earliest beginnings, its build-ers had settled themselves in a wide circle, each individual family unit building up a small, low mound which, at its base, soon began to overlap with the adjoining accumulations thus formed, until, eventually, a large ring had taken shape.

The most characteristic trait of the Puerto Hormiga complex is the pottery. The Archaic Stage is usually a pre-ceramic stage, but at Puerto Hormiga large quantities of potsherds were found in the different shell layers and pottery was already present when the first groups settled at this site. As the radiocarbon dates ob-tained from organic material associated with the sherds place this complex at the very beginning of the third millennium BC, this would be the earliest pottery anywhere in the New World, a fact which is of considerable importance. That in many parts the manufacture of ceramics preceded agriculture in the Americas is by now a well-established fact, but the exist-ence, late in the fourth millennium BC, of the potter's art in an Archaic context, in the northern Colombian lowlands, raises the problem of its origin and diffusion from there to other areas. But before discussing this wider problem, a short description must be given of the pottery and of the general cultural context within which it was found.

Two of the most common wares contain a heavy fibre temper of a type unique in South America. One of them consists of long, thin fibres, with a round cross-section, probably a grass or

Spanish moss, considerable quantities of which were added to the clay before shaping it into crude bowls. During the firing process this admixture of organic matter was carbonized and disappeared leaving innumerable tubular hollows in the baked clay and giving it a sponge-like consistency. The sherds are light and porous, and crumble easily when pressure is applied to them. Another type of fibre temper is constituted of short flat leaves, like dry grass blades crushed between the fingers. These tiny fragments did not produce hollow spaces during firing, but left their imprints in the clay, clearly showing their organic structure. The vessels manufactured of this mixture have a much stronger consistency and do not have the porous quality of the other fibre-tempered ware. The bowl-shaped or slightly ovate containers are thick-walled and poorly made, having been fired at a low temperature. Both fibre-tempered wares were manufac- tured not by the technique of superimposed coils, but apparently by direct modelling from a lump of clay. The rough, irregular, brownish or reddish surfaces of this pottery are devoid of any decoration, and the entire complex gives the impression of an initial phase of the potter's art. However, associated with this very crude pottery, there also exist two types of sand-tempered ware which show a somewhat higher technological develop- ment. Although the same bowl-shaped vessels prevail through- out the different layers of the shell-mound, some of them are decorated with shallow grooves which often contain a red ochre fill which was rubbed or painted in the depressed areas. The serrated edge of a sea-shell was used as a rocker stamp which produced closely spaced dentate marks on the surface, and some of the containers are decorated with crudely modelled zoo- morphic appendages which represent frogs or small rodents in the attitude of climbing up to the rim of the bowl. The broad, out- turned rim of a large bowl shows a partly modelled, partly in- cised, human face, with large eyes formed by several concentric circles. We have here a considerable artistic development which

Fig. 11

Plates 1, 4

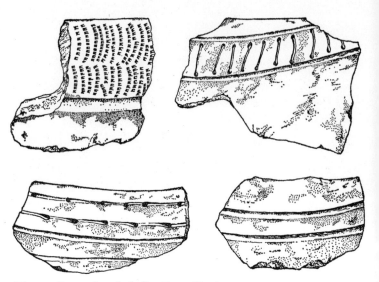

Fig. 11. Decorated potsherds from Puerto Hormiga

in spite of its crudeness already follows a well-defined style. The fact that the sand-tempered wares of this complex are rather well developed shows that this pottery is not the result of an initial stage but that its origins go back to an even earlier time-level.

A number of non-ceramic artifacts reflect, in part, the basic economy of the Puerto Hormiga folk. The gathering of molluscs was combined with small-game hunting and fishing, but it seems that these activities were limited to birds, reptiles, a few small rodents, and estuary or river species of fish; no bones of larger mammals such as deer or peccary were found. Many small anvil stones with an oval depression and accompanied by heavy hammer-stones, were used for cracking palm seeds, and the presence of stone slabs and pestles points to the use of other vegetable foods. As a matter of fact, there are many flat, thin grinding slabs, and heavy pebbles which seem to have been used for grinding or mashing roots or seeds. The Puerto Hormiga Indians were true food-gatherers, but their dietary habits

Fig. 12

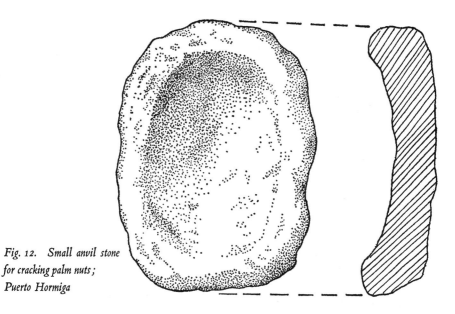

clearly include already a certain quantity of vegetable foods and
it is possible that they practised some small-seed harvesting.
Flaked pebbles and some crudely worked flakes were used as
choppers or scraping tools, but this lithic industry does not include any projectile points. Basketry or, at least, plaited mats,
were present, and impressions on clay were found in several
parts of the mound.

We know nothing at present about the origin of Puerto Hormiga pottery. The fibre-tempered wares and some of the decorated sand-tempered sherds show marked similarities with the
earliest pottery of the lower Mississippi valley and of Florida
(Orange Plain series), but there is still no proof whatsoever of a
northward diffusion of the Puerto Hormiga ceramic complex,
across Central America and the Mesoamerican area. Eventually
such evidence for diffusion may be found on the western Caribbean shore or on the Pacific coast. From Colombia toward the
east there is better evidence for diffusion. The Barrancas Phase

of the lower Orinoco river in Venezuela, beginning about 900 BC, probably derives its characteristic biomorphic and in-cised ceramic decoration from the Colombian pottery tradition originating at Puerto Hormiga. There is a dearth of evidence for specific lines of diffusion of this earliest pottery; a search for shell-fishing stations in the coastal lowlands of Central and Mesoamerica will help to clarify the problem.

This pattern of life, of the shell-fish gatherers, fishermen, and hunters of small game, continues then on the coastal lowlands of Colombia for more than twenty centuries, without any major changes or shifts in general cultural content. Sites which have produced evidence for this cultural stage are scattered over a wide area of the coast and the lagoons of the lower courses of the rivers which flow into the Caribbean. At Canapote, a suburb of Cartagena, a series of shell-mounds dating to 2000 BC were found to contain a ceramic complex quite similar to Puerto Hormiga, although by then the fibre-tempered wares have been replaced entirely by coarse sand-tempered types decorated with shallow grooves. Another group of large shell-mounds, some of them as high as 6 m., is located at Barlovento, in the swamps to the north-east of Cartagena. The excavation of these mounds brought to light a large amount of pottery, more than 20,000 sherds which, in their shapes and decorative techniques, con-tinue the Puerto Hormiga tradition. No complete pots were found but from some of the larger fragments it is possible to re-construct the shapes of the containers. Hemispherical or ovate bowls are the predominant forms, and occasionally these are

Fig. 13   provided with small lugs protruding from the rim. Simple geo-metric designs – parallel lines, curvilinear or spiral-shaped ele-ments, lines of dots, or rings impressed with a tubular imple-ment – adorn the upper part of some of the vessels, and often the shallow incisions are filled with red ochre. Among the lithic artifacts there are a number of pitted stones which show traces of fire, and which were probably used as cooking-stones. This

Fig. 13. Decorated potsherds from Barlovento

method of heating food in an open container by dropping hot stones into it seems to have been a common practice, and the poor quality of the pottery together with the lack of soot-black-ened, heavily fired basal sherds, suggests that neither at Puerto Hormiga nor among the later shell-mound dwellers was pot-tery used directly on the fire. The chronological position of the Barlovento complex has been established by a sequence of four radiocarbon dates which range from 1550 to 1032 BC, thus allowing a time-span of 500 years for the accumulation of the 6 metre-deep deposits of this site.[12]

No less interesting are a number of other sites of Barlovento type which are found on the coast north-east of Cartagena, to-ward Barranquilla, and on some of the small off-shore islands. Several large shell-mounds containing pottery of the Barlovento phase are located near the Ciénaga del Totumo, halfway be-tween the type-site and the mouth of the Magdalena river, and several smaller mounds pertaining to the same phase are on the islands of Barú and Tierra Bomba, south of Cartagena, and on the Gulf of Morrosquillo, between Cartagena and the Gulf of Urabá.

It seems that already between 3000 and 2000 BC, there was a considerable spread southward, ascending the lower course of the Magdalena, almost to the fringes of the mountains. At Bu-carelia, near Zambrano, the fibre-tempered Puerto Hormiga

Plates 2, 3

ware, this time somewhat more elaboratedly decorated and containing many new elements such as spouts and handles, appears some 150 km. inland, and a complex related to Barlovento is found as far south as the Isla de los Indios, a small islet in the lagoon of Zapatosa, at the confluence of the Magdalena and Cesar rivers.[13]

We do not know what happened in the interior provinces of Colombia at the time when the Puerto Hormiga and, later on, the Barlovento phases developed in the northern lowlands. No sites containing correspondingly early ceramic complexes have yet been found. Although we have no direct evidence, it may be that the interior was a sparsely inhabited cultural backwater during the second and third millennia BC and that the more important developments took place on the Caribbean coast.

Fig. 14.
Barbed bone
harpoon from
Bucarelia

CHAPTER V
The Early Horticulturalists

THE SHELL-MOUND DWELLERS of the coastal lowlands had been seasonal gatherers and had led a semi-
nomadic life, fishing at times, at other times collecting, revisiting
at intervals those spots where from experience they knew that
there was food and shelter. In time, a few vegetable foods had
become of importance in their diet, and on their wanderings
they carried along their flat grinding slabs and *manos,* to grind
seeds or shoots. It was during this stage of cultural development,
this stage of roaming bands which once in a while settled down
at some propitious camp-site, that plant domestication began.
Horticulture, of course, is not a sudden invention; it is a long
process developing over hundreds, perhaps thousands of years,
slowly progressing as more and more experimental knowledge
is acquired with regard to seed selection, soil properties, climatic
influences, and nutritional values and predilections. The shell-
mound dwellers must already have observed that some edible
roots or fruits thrived better under certain conditions of moisture
or in certain soils, and that stems or ratoons could be planted
and give yields according to the amount of care that accompanied the planting and the early growth stages. They did not
'invent' horticulture; they helped it develop by building upon
the experience of generations. It was the root crops which seem
to have attracted them above all others, and by domesticating
some of them they brought about a major shift in their entire
culture, in fact a profound change in the cultural development
of tropical America.

While the Barlovento phase was coming to an end around
1000 BC, in other parts of the lowlands another development
was taking place. As we have already pointed out, some groups
had begun to move south, away from the coast and, by migrating

along the rivers and to the inland lagoons, were leaving the shell-fishing grounds which, for many generations, had been their principal source of food. It is quite possible that some communities stayed on the coast and continued to gather mol- luscs on the beaches and estuaries, but the general tendency seems to have been an inland migration and the adaptation to a new physical environment: the large rivers and freshwater lagoons.

This movement away from the sea-shore and toward the south obviously implied a new ecological adaptation and it is reason- able to suppose that the impulse to this movement was brought about by the exploitation of new food resources. We believe that this change in the economic life of the coastal communities may have resulted from the adoption of a new food complex, the systematic cultivation of manioc.

The tropical lowlands of South America are the home of many edible roots and, unlike Mesoamerica and the Central Andes where seed crops such as maize and beans had already been domesticated long before the time of Christ, the tropical forest tribes were beginning to cultivate certain roots, especially some varieties of manioc, one of the many species of the genus *Manihot* which is a native of the Western Hemisphere. The large edible tubers of this shrub are an important carbohydrate source, and the plant combines many features which make it particularly attractive to simple forest-dwelling peoples: it is easily cultivated under many different climatic conditions, from semi-arid regions to rain-forest environments; propagated by stem cuttings it needs but little care, while yields are large; it is relatively resistant to pests and diseases, and it lends itself readily to various forms of hybridization. Of the cultivated species *(Manihot esculenta)* there are two kinds, the so-called 'sweet' and 'bitter' manioc, which have very similar morphological char- acteristics but are differentiated by their prussic acid content. While in the 'sweet' varieties the content is very low and they can be consumed readily raw or cooked, the HCN-containing varieties have a bitter taste and the poisonous component has to be eliminated by a special processing technique before the roots become edible. To accomplish this, the South American Indians have developed an elaborate device, the *tipití* or *sebucán*, a long sleeve-like basket which, being twilled diagonally from strong liana fibres, has great elasticity. The tubular basket stretches when filled tightly with the grated mass, after which the poisonous juice can be squeezed out by compressing the tube, generally by pulling the two ends. This, of course, is an advanced technique practised by the historical tribes of northern South America. The prehistoric horticulturalists and incipient agriculturalists who first domesticated manioc probably had some simpler devices or preferred the sweet, non-poisonous varieties which are typical of the lowlands and the subtropical regions lying to the west of the Eastern Cordillera. The use of the pressure basket is probably a later adaptation to the Amazonian rain-forest environment.[14]

Manioc (or *yuca*, as it is commonly called in Colombia) can be eaten cooked or toasted, but there are two other ways of preparing this important foodstuff: as a coarse flour *(manioco)* or as a dry, flat cake *(cazabe)*. In both food preparations the finely grated mass is spread out over a large flat griddle (a *comal*, as it is called in Mesoamerica, or *budare*, in the Amazon-Orinoco area), a disk of clay of up to 60 cm. in diameter, which is placed over an open fire; it is supported by stones or clay stands. By stirring the mass with a wooden paddle, a coarse-grained flour is obtained; this, when flattened out and left to consolidate, forms a thin circular cake. Both of these processed foods are of great economic value because the flour as well as the cakes can be stored and kept for months, thus constituting an important element of trade. However, in modern times and as early as the early sixteenth century, the Indian tribes living west of the Eastern Cordillera did *not* use or know this technique of food

63

preparation and conservation; it was confined exclusively to the Orinoco plains and the Amazon area, and some of the Antilles.

This poses an interesting problem, not only for the ethnologist and ethnobotanist, but for the archaeologist as well. The fact is that large clay griddles, such as are used in the preparation of bitter manioc, are found in archaeological contexts west of the Eastern Cordillera only at a rather early time-level, while during later developmental stages characterized by advanced agriculture, no evidence for this technique has come to light so far. From the admittedly scrappy evidence at hand, it appears then, that bitter manioc *was* used in coastal and interior Colombia, but that eventually it came to be replaced by sweet manioc, the important storage and trade complex of flour and cakes being developed later, east of the Andes, in the Orinoco-Amazon drainages. But be this as it may, the occurrence of large clay griddles of the *budare* type in archaeological sites points in general to manioc cultivation, and the economy of this root crop is, of course, a most important aspect in the reconstruction of the prehistoric cultures under consideration. Manioc was probably first cultivated by the tropical forest tribes of eastern Venezuela and it is from this latter region that the knowledge of domestication and the technological associations of this plant seem to have been introduced into northern Colombia, giving rise to a new phase of development.

This new stage is well examplified by the Malambo complex, the type site of which is located on a lagoon of the lower Magdalena river, a short distance south of the modern town of Barranquilla. The Malambo site is composed of occupational refuse spread over a wide area and formed by pottery fragments and animal remains in the shape of bones, all of this buried under a thick alluvial layer of sterile soil. Molluscs were *not* used as food, although both the neighbouring sea-shore and the freshwater lagoon abound with them. The sand-tempered, well-polished pottery is much richer in shapes and decorative techniques than

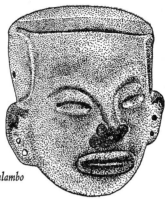

Fig. 15. Pottery mask of dark-gray clay; Malambo

that of the preceding phases; the hemispherical bowls and ovate or boat-shaped vessels continue to be used, but to these simple shapes many new ones are now added: bowls with in-curving or almost vertical walls, vessels with out-curving shoulders, flat platters or griddles, vessels with annular bases and others with supports in the form of short, foot-shaped cylinders. Many of these containers are decorated with a combination of modelling and incising. Zoomorphic lugs and appendages *(adornos)* bear parallel incised lines and grooves, and rims are often decorated with small hemispherical protuberances or appliqué pellets. A small clay mask bears witness to a considerable aesthetic ad-vance achieved during this phase. These modelled *adornos,* to-gether with the use of multiple incisions outlining and empha-sizing the prominent parts are, of course, reminiscent of the earlier decoration found at Puerto Hormiga and Bucarelia, but Malambo is technologically much more advanced and shows more varied forms. The main difference, however, between Malambo and the cultural complexes of the preceding phases lies in its economic basis. According to the radiocarbon dates from Malambo, early in the first millennium BC the pattern of shell-fish gathering and occasional vegetable consumption was gradually changing to one of root-cropping. The absence of shell accumulations and the presence of abundant griddle sherds shows this quite clearly.[15]

Fig. 15

The question now arises as to the origin of this new food crop and of the ceramic complex which accompanies its introduction into the northern Colombian lowlands. Detailed comparison of Malambo pottery with Venezuelan pottery of a similar time-level indicates that a close relationship exists between Malambo and the so-called Barrancoid Series. This pottery which developed on the lower Orinoco and eventually spread toward the Caribbean coast of Venezuela shares many similarities with the Malambo ceramics and it seems reasonable to suppose that the latter grew out of the Barrancoid tradition, introduced by manioc-farming immigrants from the Venezuelan coast. The earliest radiocarbon date for Malambo is 1120 BC, the terminal date being AD 70. This seems to be in accordance with the radiocarbon dates for Venezuela which place the Barrancoid Series in the upper part of Period II of the Venezuelan chronology, with a time-span of about 1000 to 350 BC. Furthermore, the terminal date for Barlovento is 1032 BC, making it contemporaneous with the beginnings of Malambo. However, the pots of the two sites share very few traits, Malambo being stylistically and technologically far superior to the coarse Barlovento wares. This seems to indicate that the Malambo tradition represents essentially a Venezuelan development, although the origins of the very same Venezuelan pottery were derived, almost 2,000 years earlier, from a northern Colombian source, i.e., from Puerto Hormiga.

Life on the rivers and inland lagoons was very different from that which people had led on the shell-mounds in the swamps and on the beaches. The rivers and the surrounding country offered new and plentiful resources, the efficient exploitation of which now became the mainspring of cultural advance. It was here on the rivers that a new pattern of sedentary village life was beginning to take shape, and in order to appreciate the true importance of this step, we must refer once more to the economic basis of aboriginal culture.

The many large rivers of inter-Andean Colombia are very rich in fish, certain species of which run yearly in immense quantities, such as the 'bagre' *(Pseudoplatystoma fasciatum)* and the 'bocachico' *(Prochilodus reticulatus magdalenae)*. Even today, with a dense Creole population and greatly improved fishing techniques, the rivers continue to be an almost inexhaustible source of fish of the best quality. But not less important are the rivers and swamps of the northern flood-plains for their reptiles: crocodiles, caymans, turtles and iguanas and other lizards. These regions teem with many different species of turtles, some of them very large. If we think, then, of these rivers in terms of a perennial source of proteins, we can suppose that sedentary village life in Colombia had, from its earliest beginnings, a marked riparian orientation, and that agriculture was not such a determining factor in its origins and increase as it was, for example, in the Valley of Mexico, in Guatemala, or in the Peruvian coastal valleys. As a matter of fact, such a way of life would have been quite possible with a minimum of systematic cultivation. It appears to have been freshwater fishing and reptile hunting which first gave stability to society in the Colombian tropics.[16]

This stage of development, roughly equivalent to the Old World Neolithic, has been termed the Formative Stage, and is characterized by a configuration of certain economic, technological and sociological traits. This new environmental adaptation led, first of all, to a well-defined type of settlement pattern. We now find sedentary villages, most of them still small, but some already of fairly large size, on the flat shores of lagoons or on the oxbow lakes. The concentration, variety, and considerable depth of the occupational débris, which often forms deposits several metres thick, indicate that these were the dwelling places of stable communities which had reached a high level of efficiency in the exploitation of most, or all, of the resources of their respective micro-environments. On the lower Sinú, for example, in one single trench, more than 18,000 fragments of turtle shell were recovered and in this and other sites there were huge quantities of crocodile bones, mammalian remains, and the remains of many different species of fish. At the same time, large clay griddles are a characteristic feature of the ceramic complexes in question, suggesting, together with the thin, flat grinding slabs and *manos,* that root cultivation was becoming more important.

There are many sites in the northern Colombian lowlands which are representative of this stage. They are found scattered along the Magdalena and Cauca rivers, on the Sinú and the San Jorge, on the lagoons lying in the interfluvial zones, and on the Gulf of Urabá, near the Panamanian border. A typical site, where major excavations have been carried out in recent years, is Momil, located on a large lagoon formed by the lower Sinú river, and a short description of its main characteristics is due here in order to gain a better understanding of this new and most important stage of cultural development.[17]

The Momil people, like those of the Malambo culture, lived in a sedentary village, on a flat stretch of land lying between the shore of the lagoon and a short range of low hills. The more than three metre-deep accumulation of occupational refuse, spread over an area of several hundred square metres, was found to contain an ample record of this culture. It included many thousands of potsherds (more than 300,000), lithic artifacts, objects of bone and shell, and a large quantity of food remains. Both the physical superposition and the variations in vertical distribution of the cultural remains indicate a developmental sequence with a major break at about half the depth of the deposit. On the basis of certain physical characteristics of the matrix and of vertical quantitative and qualitative distribution of pottery types, decorative techniques, and other criteria, the cultural content can be broken down into two major periods which have been designated Momil I and Momil II.

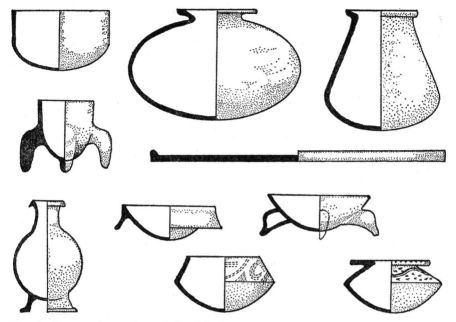

Fig. 16. Representative pottery vessels from Momil

There is, indeed, a considerable evolution from the drab, coarse pottery of the Archaic Stage to the well-finished vessels of Momil, and from the few crude hammer-stones and pestles of the shell-mound dwellers to the varied artifact typology of the sedentary horticulturalists. Characteristic vessel shapes of Momil I, that is the earliest period, include globular vessels with restricted necks and wide everted rims, hemispherical vessels with straight rims, several types of composite-silhouette bowls with a pronounced shoulder, round-bottomed and short-necked globular jars with flaring rims turned down at an angle, very large flat plates of the *budare* type with a thick raised rim, small flat griddles and slightly concave dishes with broad out-flaring rims. Some vessel shapes of Momil II carry on this earlier tradition, such as hemispherical bowls and composite-silhouette bowls with in-turned rims, but many new vessel shapes also

Fig. 16

appear. Very characteristic for Momil II are large globular storage vessels; pear-shaped vessels with out-turned rims, and
round-bottomed basal-flanged bowls, the introduction of
which coincides with the beginning of Momil II, and tripod
vessels with tall solid supports. Annular bases are present in
both periods, but low conical feet are characteristic of Momil I,
while solid or hollow mammiform supports appear only in
Momil II.

As to decorative techniques, it can be said that incised wares
still predominate throughout all levels. Dentate roulette stamping is very common in both periods. Incised wares include
shallow grooving, fine-line incision, and parallel grooving with
crosswise raked lines. Cursive curvilinear elements appear late
in Momil II, being rare in the earlier levels. Red-zoned incised
or dentate-stamped sherds with colour areas set off by incision
occur in Momil II, while stippled wares characterize Momil I,
as do appliqué strips or rows of small flat pellets stuck to the
surface. A very frequent trait of Momil I incised or roulette-
stamped wares is a white pigment filling, while a red filling is
found in the grooves on some Momil II sherds. Momil contains
some of the earliest painted pottery found in Colombia. Bichrome painting (black-on-white, black-on-red) and polychrome painting (black and red-on-white) begin in Momil I and
continue through Momil II. Both types of painted decoration
are found mainly on the inside of flat plates or the upper ex-
terior surface of bowls. For the first time in Colombian prehistory
there appears resist-dye decoration and two types can be recognized: the first occurs only in Momil I and takes the form of
irregular, badly faded grayish lines and blotches on red ware
bowls, while the second type occurs exclusively in Momil II
and shows a negative technique of black-on-red.

Next to the pottery, small, hand-modelled human figurines
are very characteristic of the Momil complex, as indeed of this
entire cultural horizon. In Momil I they are solid, crescent-based,

Plate 5

70

with handle-shaped arms and broad, flat, almost featureless heads. In Momil II there is an abrupt change; practically all figurines are hollow, some are seated, having bulbous, hollow lower extremities; others are standing on thin S-curved legs. Besides figurines, there appear a great number of miscellaneous objects of clay. Flat stamps with positive carved designs are found in Momil I, and are followed, in Momil II, by hollow cylindrical roller stamps. Zoomorphic whistles, at first rather crudely shaped but later well modelled, are typical for Momil II, but absent in Momil I. Bar-shaped clay pendants, pottery rattles with cylindrical handles, and well-polished unperforated disks with complex designs engraved upon one face only, are all representative of Momil I. A double-faced *adorno* suggesting a concept of dualism comes from the bottom levels of Momil II. Spherical spindle whorls were found in the upper levels of the same period. Biomorphic modelled *adornos,* some of them re-presenting birds' heads, are frequent in Momil II but lacking in Momil I.

Objects of stone are abundant in both periods. Momil I is characterized by a flint industry with both percussion and pres-sure flaking in evidence. No core tools were found, but several nuclei with prepared striking platforms are present. Simple side scrapers and microlithic drills are common, the latter having an approximately hexagonal or rectangular cross-section, with secondary retouching along the edges. Many of them have di-minutive stems and the entire object is about one centimetre long. The many small splinters of flint which are found in the refuse were probably set into grating-boards of wood, such as are still used by the Amazonian Indians for grating manioc. Abrading and polishing tools of sandstone or calcareous mate-rial appear in many different shapes. Pebble tools, hammer-stones, or miscellaneous polished and flaked fragments are com-mon in both periods. Of special importance, however, is the fact that flat or trough-shaped *metates,* i.e., grinding stones, and loaf-shaped *manos* appear only from the bottom levels of Momil II upwards. Objects of shell are represented among others by *Strombus* picks, cups, spoons, buttons, *Oliva* tinklers, and *Venus* shells with a perforated apex. A number of bone awls, eyeless needles, antler tools, disks, and miscellaneous bone fragments with cuts, perforations, or polished surfaces were found in both periods. The occurrence of clay and bone spindle whorls points to the knowledge of weaving cotton cloth. Throughout the whole sequence thousands of fragments of turtle shell, mammal bones, and fish remains were found; sea and freshwater molluscs seem to have been used only for purposes of manufacturing tools or ornaments from their shells, but not as food.

This detailed description may have been hard going for some readers but it is justified in view of the importance of this site. Taking the Momil complex as a starting point, we must now examine the economic and sociological aspects of this wide-spread cultural stage, together with its external relationships. There can be no doubt about the sedentary nature of society at this stage of development, based upon an efficient combination of horticulture and riverine resources. However, Momil (and other sites, too) shows an important sequence in this develop-ment of basic economic resources. In Momil I there is no clear evidence of seed planting; heavy grinding stones *(metates)* and mullers appearing quite suddenly in Momil II. But Momil I is dominated by a very characteristic element which seems to be associated with manioc: the large, flat circular griddle with a sharply raised rim. In the preparation of foods based upon maize this type of rim has little or no function, but in the case of manioc flour it is a necessity.

This would suggest that Momil, and the general develop-mental stage of which this site forms part, is representative of the transition from root cropping to maize cultivation. Such a step, of course, consists not only in the replacement of one staple food by another but, first of all, in a total change of agricultural procedure, namely the step from vegetative reproduction, i.e., the planting of stem cuttings, to seed agriculture and everything this latter concept implies in terms of knowledge of soil properties and preparation, seed selection, cycles of growth, etc. Maize was first domesticated in Mexico, where the earliest cultivated types date from about 3500 BC. But the use of this all-important food plant spread only much later to South America, not reaching the Peruvian coast until the end of the second millennium BC. In Colombia, as we have seen, there is no evidence for maize cultivation in the northern lowlands during Puerto Hormiga, Barlovento or Malambo times, nor even during the earlier stages of the Momil sequence, when horticulture was already fairly well developed. Only with the beginning of Momil II do we find the characteristic grinding implements and the pottery shapes usually associated with maize agriculture: the trough-shaped *metates,* the loaf-shaped *manos,* small griddles for toasting the flat cakes (the Mexican *tortilla,* or *arepa,* as it is called in Colombia), large storage vessels for maize beer, and others. Momil I, as we have pointed out, lacks these elements but yields an abundance of large toasting plates and scraping tools of stone, which are rather indicative of root horticulture. Of course, inferences from pottery shapes or other implements as to the use of certain food plants can be misleading, and the absence of grinding stones and *manos* at a particular site does not necessarily prove ignorance or absence of maize cultivation. The same can be said about manioc, which occasionally can be prepared for consumption without the aid of large toasting plates. However, the vertical distribution of the pottery and stone implements at Momil is striking in this respect, and the hypothesis of a manioc-maize sequence in Momil I and II is also strengthened by some additional evidence. In the first place, the appearance of large grinding stones and mullers in Momil II is clearly accompanied by the introduction of a series of new traits which are highly suggestive of Mesoamerican influence, such as bowls

with flanged bases, tall tripod vessels, bulbous mammiform supports, and bird-shaped whistles. It seems that maize was introduced at this time-level from Mesoamerica as a fully developed
complex together with a number of new pottery shapes. In the
second place, evidence for a similar manioc-maize sequence
has been obtained from Venezuela, and the sites providing it
are related to Colombian sites. The time sequence of the two
basic American agricultural systems, the seed planters of Mesoamerica and the root planters of tropical South America, had
previously been postulated by the plant geographers; it is now
being borne out by archaeological research.

An important point still remains to be discussed while we are
on the subject of the economic basis of the Colombian Formative cultures, namely the relatively late date at which maize
cultivation was adopted by the early horticulturalists of the
northern lowlands. The answer seems to be, in part at least, that
the dietary needs of these early villagers were amply met by their
combination of starchy roots, animal proteins and fats obtained
from riverine resources, and that this alimentary basis did not
make maize a highly desirable food. However, with an enlarging population and, perhaps, slowly diminishing protein
sources, maize was accepted to redress the dietary balance. An
additional reason for the rather late and sudden acceptance of
maize farming lies in a marked climatic change which,
according to recent pollen analyses, occurred in the northern
lowlands. Around 700 BC the prevailing dry and continental
climate of the coast seems to have turned more humid with
increasing rainfall. This, of course, provided the environmental
setting necessary for efficient maize cultivation and may well
have been a decisive factor in the rapid spread of this new food
plant. What is more, the introduction of a fully developed maize
complex may well have been brought about by a new people
penetrating into Colombia from the outside, most probably
from Mesoamerica. We shall enlarge on this later.[18]

Before we go any further in our search for the traces of the Colombian Indian's environmental adaptation and cultural evolution, we must return once more to Momil and try to evaluate some of the social consequences of increased food production and the ensuing population growth. In many ways, the development from root agriculture to efficient seed planting constitutes a crucial point for the social structure of the communities involved. Roots like manioc cannot be stored for any length of time for future use. They have to be consumed as soon as they are dug out of the ground, and they spoil if left too long underground. The root horticulturalist or the fisherman cannot easily accumulate a large surplus and store food to be consumed during periods when he might devote his energies to other activities not directly oriented toward mere subsistence. The maize farmer is in a far better position. With two, or even three harvests a year and a minimum time spent on the care of his crop, he can gather a large quantity of seeds which are easy to store, to trade, or to convert into a number of palatable dishes. There is, then, a considerable difference between the man who tends his root crop all year round and the man who has a storage bin full of maize and can now pursue other activities. Maize cultivation probably plays an important role in the social organization of the community.

No burials have been found at Momil which would indicate a differential treatment of the dead, but there is some evidence for craft specialization. The similarity or near-identity of many decorated vessels, figurines or other artifacts suggest the presence of skilled potters who produced series of their wares for their customers. Besides, the differences to be observed in the quality of personal adornments such as necklace beads, pendants, or those represented on anthropomorphic clay figurines, also indicate possible status differences. Momil probably saw the beginnings of a stratified society and the slow rise of a class of leaders and specialists in different arts and crafts.

As has been mentioned earlier, very characteristic of Momil are the many small anthropomorphic figurines of clay, some 1,700 specimens of which were found at this site. In Momil these figurines make their first appearance in a total complex but it is quite possible that they were developed at an earlier time level. In any case, anthropomorphic effigies of different shapes and styles are fairly characteristic of many Formative sites, from Mexico to Ecuador, as well as in other areas. They are generally found scattered in the miscellaneous debris of household refuse accumulations, and many theories have been advanced to ex-plain their possible function and the uses to which these objects were put by the native cultures responsible for them. Some au-thors take them to be simple toys, but others are inclined to see in them ceremonial objects connected with fertility rites. This may be true for certain cultural contexts, but in the case of Co-lombia the alternative explanation might be offered that these figurines were used in curing rituals. Quite frequently these human effigies portray people with physical handicaps or ab-normalities. There are hunchbacks, pregnant women, faces with 'weeping eyes', or persons grasping the head with both hands. Disease and physical discomfort in their widest sense – including such phenomena as menstruation, pregnancy, tooth-aches, headaches, stomach complaints, etc. – may well have been recurrent occasions for institutionalized crisis rites when a certain set of material objects were used which, once they had performed their brief function, were discarded, only to be made anew when another curing ritual was prepared. Among the modern Chocó and Cuna Indians of western Colombia, a set of wooden figurines forms an essential part of all shamanistic practices connected with the curing and prevention of disease. Once the ritual is over, these figurines lose their magic power and are simply thrown away. If this ethnographic correlation is valid and if the hypothesis that many of the archaeological clay figurines found in Formative sites were used in disease-curing

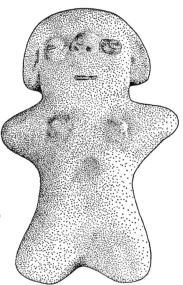

Fig. 17. Anthropomorphic clay figurine from Ciénaga de Oro

or preventive ritual, a large assemblage of associated 'problem-atic' artifacts would become more intelligible; for example, the clay rattles, pottery whistles, miniature vessels, pottery drums, and a variety of other small objects which are found so frequent-ly in sites containing figurines and which might have formed part of this ritual complex. But be this as it may, the small an-thropomorphic figurines found at many Formative sites of trop-ical Colombia represent an important aboriginal art form and are probably among the first evidences of shamanistic practices among the early agricultural peoples.[19]

Cannibalism, another trait of probably ritualistic signifi-cance, also makes its first appearance in Momil. In this case the evidence is provided by disjointed human bones which are found scattered in the refuse and which certainly do not pertain to burials.

Although no metal objects were found at the Momil site, it seems probable that gold-work was present at this general time level. At Ciénaga de Oro, a large site closely related to Momil, small tubular beads of hammered gold have been found, and

Fig. 17
Plate 6

77

the same is true of several other sites forming part of the Momil complex.

We must turn now to the problem of the external relation-ships of Momil. On the northern coast its presence is well estab-lished by several sites, all of them in a very similar environment of rivers and lagoons. But in the inter-Andean valleys very little evidence for this complex has so far come to light. Again, as in the case of the preceding phases, this may be due to the general lack of systematic exploration in these regions, but it also seems possible that, at this time period, large parts of the Andean in-terior still remained sparsely or intermittently settled. The north-ern lowlands probably provided a more propitious environment for this level of technology and ecological adaptiveness than the rugged mountain slopes of the Andean system.

We have no absolute dates for Momil and so its chronological position can only be arrived at by comparing its artifacts with those of dated cultures. Such culture complexes are found above all in the Mesoamerican area and are there generally comparable with Formative developments of the first and the later half of the second millennium BC. Such sites as Tlatilco in Mexico, Playa de los Muertos and Yarumela in Honduras, and many others occupying a similar time position, share with Momil a signifi-cant number of traits. A short list of the most characteristic similarities – both in form and in decoration – shows this rela-tionship: bowls with flanges at the base, mammiform supports, tall solid tripods, tubular spouts, red-zoned incision, shallow grooving, decorated rims with a roughly Z-shaped profile, pig-ment filling in incised lines, anthropomorphic figurines, flat and cylindrical stamps, zoomorphic whistles, vertically grooved ves-sels, and so on. As has been pointed out already, this Meso-american influence accompanies the introduction of the maize complex.

The rather sudden emergence of the Momil complex, together with its Mesoamerican relationships, gives rise to several questions which in the present state of knowledge cannot yet be answered in a perfectly satisfactory manner. From Puerto Hormiga to Malambo times the development had been gradual, one phase merging slowly into the next, ceramic styles being easily traceable and subsistence patterns evolving in a recognizable way. But Momil is different; there is no clear-cut local background to it, neither in its pottery and other clay artifacts, nor in its lithic assemblages. The entire complex is so rich and varied, so full of small, well-made artifacts, that one wonders what were its local antecedents. There are similarities with Malambo – some pottery shapes, the broad-line incisions and biomorphic modelling and, of course, the general economic basis – but Momil reaches a much higher technological level and, if we may judge from the figurine complex, a more developed religious system. There is a break between Malambo and Momil, not so much in a chronological sense as in total content and emphasis. The well-defined style in figurines, in painted decoration, in small clay objects, and in the manufacture of microliths, has no local precedents.

It is quite possible that we simply have not yet found the sites containing the transitional phases or the local roots of Momil culture, but from the available evidence it would appear that Momil represents a new cultural influx, the carriers of which arrived on the coastal plains from the outside. We must leave these questions unanswered. All we know is that the subsistence and settlement patterns of Momil, its ceramic style and technology, spread over large regions of the coast, providing a new impetus and giving rise to new phases whose local characteristics we shall describe in a later chapter. Until then we must keep in mind that 'mesoamericanizing' influences are beginning to re-shape the local traditions and that maize farming is from now on providing the foundations for most of the future developments.

CHAPTER VI

The Rise of the Sub-Andean Cultures

THE INTRODUCTION and consequent rapid spread of maize farming had a far-reaching influence upon the early horticulturalists of the lowlands. The high nutritional value of maize, together with its adaptability to different soils, altitudes, and climatic conditions, now made it much easier for the lowland Indians to penetrate the interior and to settle on mountain slopes and hill-tops, away from the rivers and lagoons. As a matter of fact, it seems to have been maize farming that brought about the rapid expansion of an enlarging population over the flanks of the Colombian mountain systems, a region which, until then, was probably little more than a sparsely inhabited hunting territory or the habitat of small-scale communities of incipient horticulturalists. This new ecological adaptation led to the development of a settlement pattern now characterized by decentralization. The compact riparian villages were abandoned; the growing population began to spread over the tropical and sub-tropical mountain slopes where they built scattered houses, sometimes singly, sometimes in groups of three or four, wherever the broken terrain was propitious for the establishment of small farms.

The new trend toward the mountain valleys did not, of course, lead to the abandonment of the lowlands; large groups remained behind and continued their former way of life, but the general shift was toward the interior, to the valleys of the three cordilleras. Among the most notable consequences of this new trend a few stand out; these, because of their particular cultural importance, must be dealt here in more detail. In the first place, the move into the mountainous interior must have given a powerful impetus to agricultural techniques and experimentation. Colombia occupies a most important place in the field of plant domestication and diversification of native cultigens, and the innumerable micro-environments, varying in altitude, soil characteristics, and meteorological factors, were an ideal laboratory for this purpose. A considerable amount of experimentation with new plants, or new varieties of already domesticated ones, must by this time have begun in the lowlands, and the domestication of certain root crops which thrive in regions of low or irregular precipitation had led to the sporadic settling of interfluvial regions, but once definite independence of a riverine environment had been made possible through maize farming, the newly occupied land added a great many stimuli to the intensification and – above all, diversification – of agricultural practices. Now, maize cultivation, if it is to be profitable, requires a great deal of rain and sunshine, but productivity depends not so much on their quantity as on their seasonal distribution. To a certain degree, the specific requirements of this crop which in itself is, of course, a cultural product, led the way to those regions where productivity was great because of a particularly favourable combination of physiographic and meteorological factors. At the same time, this environment favoured a wide range of other highly productive food plants, a great variety of which could be cultivated on the fertile temperate slopes of the cordilleras. Within this new environmental potential we now find the germ of a changing pattern of life. Maize-farming communities were establishing themselves over wide areas of the mountains, following the valleys of the Cauca and Magdalena rivers, and colonizing the flanks of the Andes.

A second consequence of the spread of the maize farmers was of no less importance than their expanding agricultural knowledge. Life in the intermontane basins, the narrow valleys, or the cool highland plateaux was marked by regionalism and cultural isolation. In the coastal lowlands there had always been a common denominator in terms of similar climatic conditions and of an over-all economic system based on riverine or sea

resources, but now this former unity was disappearing. Adaptation to the individual micro-environments brought about diversification and the growth of local cultures which, although
sometimes they occupied neighbouring valleys, differed widely
in their scope and content. There were no 'co-traditions' nor
'horizon-styles' comparable with those found in the Central
Andes, but a marked diversity due to geographic and cultural
isolation, and due to different ways of coping with the local
environment.[20]

We must examine more closely the archaeological record left
behind by the maize-farming communities which, around the
time of Christ, peopled the mountainous interior of Colombia.
As far as one can judge from the present state of archaeological
knowledge, the pattern of decentralization prevailed over wide
areas. On the northernmost spurs of the three cordilleras, on the
flanks of the Magdalena and Cauca valleys, and in the Andean
core-land, small sites are found scattered and in isolation, at
different altitudes. To a people used to living on plains and
river banks, the new slope environment posed certain technological problems in their domestic architecture. To find level
ground for a house site was often difficult and so a piece of flat
ground had to be prepared by a combined technique of cut and
fill. These small, round, or more often crescent-shaped, house
sites are very characteristic for the slope dwellers, and associated
with them one often finds stone alignments, enclosing circles of
irregular blocks, or rudimentary retaining walls surrounding
parts of the house platform. We have here, then, an incipient
stage of architecture which, although it subsequently develops
to a very limited extent, becomes a frequent feature of the slope-
dwelling maize farmers. Large, heavy *metates* and *manos* are
found on these sites, within the hut foundations or in the *patio*
(the flat stretch of ground surrounding the house), and there are
sometimes bedrock mortars deeply hollowed-out on the flat surface of outcrops or on large boulders. The coarse but well-made

pottery is generally sand-tempered although occasionally ground sherds are used as a tempering material, especially in the central provinces. On the coast shell-temper occurs, often in combina-tion with fine sand. Most of the vessels are fired in an oxidizing atmosphere, having a reddish-brown colour, but black wares do occur in some instances. There is a great variety of forms: annular bases and high pedestal supports are frequent; there are tubular spouts, a large variety of handles, lugs, and rim profiles, and there are many vessels with composite silhouettes. The main decorative device continues to be incision, the designs cover-ing the upper portion or the neck of the vessel, but modelling, appliqué pellets and strips, and painted decoration are also pre-sent. Large storage vessels for water are common except on sites adjacent to a stream, and similar vessels were probably used for the storage of maize beer. Human clay figurines are very scarce now, but anthropomorphic vessels of many different types are becoming more and more popular. Heavy trapezoidal stone axes of simple Neolithic type are very common, as are disk-shaped or spherical spindle whorls of clay, necklace beads of perforated stone, and other small personal adornments. It is pos-sible that urn burial began to spread at this stage, large storage vessels being used at first; but later, large ovoid or cylindrical urns were made for this specific purpose.

It would be a mistake to generalize for the whole of Colom-bia or even for restricted areas such as the Magdalena valley or the Central Cordillera, because regional differences in culture content are so marked that any over-all correlations would be extremely doubtful. Besides, for many of the interior provinces there is still a dearth of detailed information on sites and site contents excavated under controlled conditions. We must there-fore limit our appraisal to a few key regions where major ex-cavations have been carried out and where there exists a body of data pertaining, in part at least, to the cultural developments discussed in this chapter. However, before we turn to the description of specific regions and sites, we must consider first certain new developments, this time on the Pacific coast.

By about 500 BC, but probably at an even earlier date, a new cultural influence had made itself felt in the southern half of the Pacific Lowlands, more or less between the mouth of the San Juan river and the offshore island of Tumaco, near the present border of Ecuador. There can be no doubt that this new culture (or cultures) did not develop out of an older local tradition but derived from a foreign source lying outside Colombia. There appears at this time a well-defined complex which shows close similarities with early Mesoamerican developments, specifically those of the Mexican Gulf area. As there is no evidence at all for the bearers of this culture having come overland by way of the Panamanian isthmus and the Darien region, we must conclude that their southward penetration was accomplished by rafts or sea-going canoes which coasted along the shores of north-western South America. These sea-faring peoples established small colonies on the estuaries and off-shore islands, and some of them went up the rivers toward the Western Cordillera. While in the north, on the San Juan river and in the Buenaventura region, their initial influence is weak, toward the south this influence increases, and in the delta of the Patía river and the Tumaco area there are numerous sites which testify to the rapid spread of the new settlers. The available radiocarbon dates place this intrusion in the period from about 500 BC to the first century AD, and from the associated materials it appears that this Mesoamerican influence arrived in several waves and that there existed far-flung connections for long periods. The elements introduced by the new settlers show that they had brought with them a more highly developed culture than the one which had prevailed in Colombia until then. The most characteristic pottery traits are: very finely made thin-walled bowls with hollow mammiform supports, vessels with bridged double spouts; vessels with undulating peripherical, sublabial, or basal flanges;

vessels with thin pointed supports; red or brown-slipped wares with finely incised geometric designs; white-on-red painting, and anthropomorphic figurines. The large *metates* and *manos* they used point to a developed maize complex.

Since we shall be describing this culture and its sequence in more detail in another chapter, we shall refer here only to the impact caused by this outside influence. The fact that the settle-ments increase in number and depth of accumulation toward the south is most probably due to the very limited agricultural potential of the Chocó, where the high rainfall and the leached-out soils are serious obstacles to sedentary life. To a group of advanced agriculturalists the north coast and the immense man-grove swamps south of Buenaventura must have appeared as very inhospitable, and so they pushed on southward to the some-what less rainy region of Tumaco and the still more inviting coast of Ecuador. However, there was also an eastward penetra-tion, ascending the rivers and crossing the low Western Cordil-lera, and it is this movement, away from the coast and toward the Colombian interior, which is here of utmost importance. Small villages were spreading up the Mira and Patía rivers. By the middle of the third century BC, we find a village site at Ca-tanguero, on the Calima river, a tributary of the San Juan, and this site is of major importance because it establishes the first clear link with the Cauca valley. At Catanguero we find the same thin, red-slipped and incised pottery, the same undulating sublabial flanges, and the anthropomorphic figurines so char-acteristic of the coastal sites of the very same period. There is, then, a marked eastward trend, and when turning now to the major archaeological regions and individual sites of the interior, we must bear in mind this new influence from the coast and its derivation from Mesoamerica, which entered Colombia through the 'back door'.

Situated on the eastern flanks of the mountain massif from which the three cordilleras fan out toward the north, on the headwaters of the Magdalena river, lies the vil'age of San Agus' tín which has given its name to Colombia's most publicized though still little'known archaeological culture, the beginnings of which go back to the sixth century BC, or even earlier.[21] The surrounding country is one of rolling hills interspersed here and there with higher peaks and forest'covered ranges, with only a few open valleys. Lying at an altitude of some 1,700 m. above sea level, the modern village of San Agustín has a pleasant climate and the rich soil of the well'watered valley floors and mountain slopes have made it an agricultural centre of some local importance. In the immediate vicinity of the village and farther afield, scattered over hills and valleys, there exist abun' dant traces of a prehistoric people – architectural monuments, mounds, tombs, statues, and many other remains which, in the voluminous literature dealing with this area, have come to be designated the San Agustín culture. The archaeological surface remains explored so far cover an area of several hundred square kilometres and thus form a major focus of prehistoric cultural developments in north'western South America.

Although the San Agustín region was explored and con' quered around the middle of the sixteenth century by Spanish troops, who found it to be inhabited by a forest'dwelling tribe which certainly did not represent the descendants of the creators of this archaeological culture, no mention of the spectacular stone monuments is made in the ancient chronicles. The first description is found in a book by the Spanish Friar Juan de Santa Gertrudis, who visited the region in 1757. Friar Juan reports that he met there a Catholic priest from the city of Po' payán, an important Spanish colonial centre in the Cauca val' ley, who was digging eagerly for buried treasure in graves and mounds.[22] It was probably thanks to the digging and looting engaged in by this man and later treasure'hunters that most of the monuments now known were unearthed, and if the earlier chroniclers do not refer to them, this may be because all ar' chaeological remains were then covered with earth and deep tangled forest. Some forty years later, in 1797, the Colombian *savant* Francisco José de Caldas, visited the site and published a short description of it in a treatise on the geography of this region. In the course of the nineteenth century, Colombian, French, English, Italian, and German travellers visited San Agustín and they mention the archaeological sites in their reports, but no systematic research was undertaken till the German archaeologist Konrad Theodor Preuss worked at the site from 1913 to 1914. Today still, Preuss's scholarly and well-illustrated two-volume work remains the basic source on the archaeology of San Agustín and contains the first scientific account of the excavations carried out at the site. In 1935, the Colombian Ministry of Education purchased a large tract of land in order to put the principal ruins under government protection, thus establishing the 'Archaeological Park', as it is still called. In 1936–37, the first official Colombian excavations were carried out under José Pérez de Barradas, and ever since, sporadic work has been carried out there by both Colombian and foreign scholars.

Although it is evident that, of all prehistoric sites in the country, San Agustín has received the most attention, the results of this activity are not entirely satisfactory. It seems that the amount of money spent, and the number of pages written on San Agustín, are rather disproportionate to the sum of knowledge gained during this work. The search for more statues and temples has, at times, obscured the main problems of stratigraphy and typology, and even now, after years of digging, the major questions of origins, chronology, and external relationships are largely a matter for conjecture.

In the general area of San Agustín, some thirty major sites have been discovered, being referred to in the literature by local place names. Among the more important sites are: Las Mesitas, Alto de Lavapatas, Alto de Lavaderos, Alto de los Idolos,

Fig. 18

Quinchana, and El Vegón, but undoubtedly many more are still hidden in the forest or underground. The main archaeological features found at these sites are earthen mounds, megalithic temples and shrines, tombs and sepulchral chambers, and large monolithic statues. The mounds, some of which attain a diameter of 30 m. and a height of up to 5 m., consist of heaped-up earth which covers one or more temple-like structures of large stone slabs and which contain statues or stone sarcophagi. The ground plan of these temples is generally rectangular and the interior, measuring some 3 by 4 m., is roofed by one or more heavy slabs. The walls consist of slabs vertically embedded in the ground and these, together with massive stone uprights and caryatids, hold up the roof. Some of the smaller stone-lined shelters or subterranean galleries have been described as shrines and are thought to have been places of worship and not of burial. The material used in these and in most other structures or stone carvings is basalt or andesite, rocks which are common throughout the area. The slabs are simply split or only roughly dressed so that the walls show wide interstices and the whole structure takes on a dolmen-like appearance. The inside surfaces of these temples or burial chambers sometimes bear traces of geometric designs painted in dull colours. There can be no doubt that these structures were places of worship and of a cult of the dead, and indeed it seems that those who built them were concerned above all with providing their dead and their ancestors with fitting abodes, under the tutelage of their gods.

A great number of different grave types exist at San Agustín. Some are simple pits where the corpse was buried in a flexed position, accompanied by a few grave goods such as jars or a necklace of stone beads. Others are stone-built cists constructed of flat slabs set vertically in a rectangle and covering the box-like structure. Then there are deep shaft graves with vaulted lateral chambers cut into the hard soil; multiple burials in large pits; large monolithic sarcophagi weighing tons, sometimes provided

Fig. 18. Carved stone statue from San Agustín

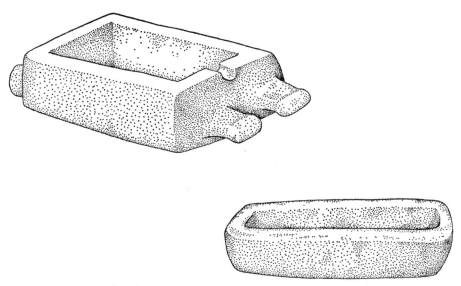

Fig. 19. Two types of monolithic sarcophagi from San Agustín

with protruding cylindrical handles and with carved lids representing the dead man. Urn burials have been found occasionally, and there is some evidence for cremation and secondary
burial rites. Corpses were buried in an extended or flexed position, sometimes even standing upright in a grave shaft, at other
times in groups lying in disorder in pits.

The San Agustín culture is probably best known for its stone
carvings, principally its statues – the monumental fierceness of
which never fails to impress those who behold them. Some
carvings in bas-relief are found on natural rock surfaces and
large boulders, and depict human beings, frogs, lizards or large
mammals. The carved covers of monolithic sarcophagi have
been mentioned above. Another type of stone carving takes the
form of roughly hewn columns, approximately cylindrical in
shape, with the outlines of a human figure – face and limbs –
lightly carved on the surface. The 'classic' type of statue, however, is represented by human or demonic figures carved in the

Fig. 19

Fig. 20
Fig. 21

Plate 7

Fig. 20.
A carved boulder;
San Agustín

round, in a highly advanced technique. As a rule, the heads are disproportionately large, the body is squat and thick-set, the limbs short and rigid. The most elaborate part is the face which often shows a very large mouth or beast-like snout, with long pointed fangs or with a protruding tongue. Half men, half felines, these statues are adorned with necklaces and bracelets; some of them hold maces or sceptres in their hands, others carry head trophies and clubs. Other body ornaments include penis cords, loin cloths or short skirts, leg bands, ear plugs, nose pendants; head ornaments in the shape of caps, wreaths or bands, and a great many other details carved in relief or incised in the surface. Quite remarkable are the different ways of representing the human eye: circular, square, almond-shaped or suggested only by a straight slit. It is possible that some of the statues represent masked figures. On several other statues we find a so-called *alter ego* representation, a secondary figure crouching on top of the head or shown as if climbing over the back and

Plates 8–11

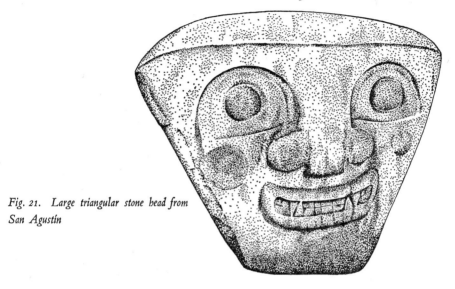

Fig. 21. Large triangular stone head from San Agustín

shoulders of the statue. While some of the images are highly stylized showing the human form in contorted outlines, others are very realistic, but the over-all impression is always one of stiffness and symmetry.

The more than 320 known statues, the tallest of which exceeds 4 m. in height, have been variously interpreted as chieftains, warriors, priests, ancestral spirits or tribal deities. The frequent representation of feline features suggests a jaguar cult, and the snakes, lizards, toads, monkeys, and birds of prey may have been lesser deities, bush spirits, or ancestral images. The statues and other rock carvings were made with crude stone celts, hundreds of which have been found discarded at the foot of some of these monuments. Several of the anthropomorphic monoliths still bear traces of polychrome painting in black, white, red and yellow.

On a rocky cliff at the Alto de Lavapatas, the Pérez de Barradas expedition discovered an intricate carving on the surface of flat boulders lying in a stream bed. Three square pools had been cut out of the rock and were connected by a series of meandering channels which distribute the water in such a way that it cascades into the basins. The rock surface is adorned with a maze of relief figures of snakes, lizards, and other animals, and human faces or whole figures wearing high head-dresses are carved on the walls, all bathed by the clear mountain stream.

Most excavators have concentrated on the ceremonial aspects of the local culture and very little work has been done on the domestic architecture of the ancient inhabitants. So far, only a few house sites have been dug, and these proved to be very simple structures in which no stones had been employed. The post-holes found in the stamped earth floor suggest small circular constructions some 3 m. in diameter, set close together in groups. The walls were probably of wattle-and-daub, and the conical roofs would have been thatched with palm leaves or mountain grass. Quite probably there are many more house sites and refuse accumulations scattered all over the area, but no systematic work has been done yet on this aspect of the San Agustín culture.

Because of this emphasis on ceremonial features, pottery analysis has been badly neglected, and our knowledge of local wares, their typology and distribution in time and space, is woefully inadequate. No individual ware types have been established yet, nor has there been any suggestion of ceramic sequences, so that we must limit our appraisal of the local pottery to an over-all description of its outstanding traits. The commonest shapes are large globular or sub-globular vessels, many of them with a pronounced slope below the sharp shoulder and characterized by a great variety of rim profiles. Smaller vessels are of similar shapes, and there are some cylindrical vessels, containers with restricted orifices, cups, bowls with high pedestal bases, shallow plates, and large deep dishes with rounded bases and slightly in-curving walls. A rather characteristic form is the coarse tripod vessel, from 15 to 35 cm. in height, the globular body of the container resting on three solid tapering legs. Sub-globular double-spouted vessels, the slightly divergent tubular spouts being connected by a flat bridge, constitute another well-defined form. Flat toasting plates provided with low vertical rims also occur, as do many types of open bowls and composite-silhouette vessels. The colour of these vessels is generally brown, red, or slightly orange, most of them having been fired in an oxidizing atmosphere. Decorations consist mainly of incised geometric designs such as parallel lines, triangles, or rows of dots; some of the larger vessels have fingertip-pressed rims. A white or red paste is frequently used as a fill in deeply incised lines. Two-colour negative and two-colour positive painting, generally black-on-red, is used on some vessels, and the designs executed in this medium are simple circles or triangles. Occasionally the coil marks of the vessel construction are left on the outside and produce a corrugated effect. There are almost no biomorphic designs on the pottery, and handles are absent except for some small lug-shaped appendages. Sand or ground sherds are common as tempering materials.

Other artifacts commonly found in excavations are large rectangular *metates,* elongated loaf-shaped *manos* and pestles, polished stone celts, obsidian chips, and a variety of unspecialized flakes which were used as scrapers or knives. In several of the graves, especially the more elaborate ones, gold objects have been found. Crescent-shaped nose ornaments cut from a hammered sheet, and also ear pendants and small necklace beads are found occasionally, but their exact associations have not been ascertained.

It is difficult to interpret the stone structures, the statues, the pottery, and the other associated features, in terms of a culture complex because too many important details are still missing in the general picture of San Agustín culture. The differences in grave types have been interpreted as indicating social stratification rather than chronological significance, and the fact that gold ornaments have been found only in well-made tombs, being absent from the simpler ones, has been adduced as additional proof of a hierarchical society. There can be no doubt that the ancient inhabitants were agriculturalists and maize farmers; the many grinding implements and some of the common pottery forms point to this. On several mountain flanks of the surrounding region (Quinchana, Quebradillas, San José de Isnos), long parallel ridges or *eras,* separated by furrows, can be observed running up and down the slopes, and it seems likely that they constitute remains of ancient fields and of an advanced agricultural technique. In any case San Agustín, at its highest cultural development, was certainly an efficient agricultural society, with a fairly dense population, craft specialization, and a highly developed religious structure.

The main problems of San Agustín are its time-depth, its chronological position, and its external relationships. On the evidence of his excavations and a series of radiocarbon dates, Luis Duque Gómez, the Colombian specialist in San Agustín archaeology, has proposed recently a sequence of three 'periods': Lower, Middle and Upper Mesitas.[23] According to this classification, the earlier period, lasting more or less from 555 BC to AD 425, is characterized by the following elements: shaft graves with side chambers, wooden coffins, wooden sculpture(?), the beginnings of gold-work; bark cloth, maize and root agriculture. The pottery forms and decoration are given as pedestal bowls, dishes, globular vessels, tripods, double-spouted vessels, composite-silhouette vessels, predominantly incised decoration, monochrome and bichrome painting, negative painting. The middle period lasted, according to Duque, from about AD 425 to 1180, being characterized by burial mounds, monolithic sarcophagi, stone cist graves, secondary urn burial, cremation, statuary, and the formation of the ceremonial necropolis pattern. The pottery tradition continues but double-spouted

vessels and tripods are absent. Advanced metallurgical techniques such as hollow casting in the *cire-perdue* technique, wire-
work, sheathing, and others are added. The third period, lasting from the twelfth century to an unknown later date, is said
to be characterized by realistic stone sculpture, circular houses,
stamped and cross-hatched pottery, loom weaving, and some
other features. Since the detailed evidence for this sequence is
still unpublished, it is difficult to assess its significance, but the
fact remains that – if the radiocarbon dates are correct – San
Agustín has a time-depth of more than 1,500 years, and that
its earlier developmental phases fall within the Formative Stage.
The question arises: What are the exact affiliations of this culture and of its different phases, and from what sources did it
derive its particular characteristics?

We must turn first to the immediate problem of the local range
of San Agustín sculpture. Stone carvings of San Agustín type
have been reported from various parts of an area including Popayán to the north and the head-waters of the Caquetá river to
the south.[24] Monolithic sarcophagi have been reported from
several parts of the Central Cordillera, and three sarcophagi of
San Agustín type have been found at Concordia, in the north
of the Cauca valley. Two large stone head tenons were found
at Cali, and from the Calima region, to the north of Cali,
a large anthropomorphic statue has been described. Many
smaller statues have been found near Pasto, in the Nariño district, and others are known from regions as far away as the highlands of the Eastern Cordillera and the foot-hills of the Sierra
Nevada of Santa Marta. It is true that in many instances there
are no stylistic resemblances, yet the fact that such concepts as
monolithic sarcophagi and large-sized anthropomorphic statues are found over so wide an area may be explained best in
terms of diffusion.

But before going any further, it is necessary to refer first to
several other archaeological cultures which have been found on

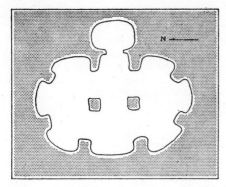
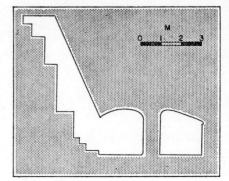

Fig. 22.   Ground-plan and cross-section of sepulchral chamber; Tierradentro

the upper Magdalena river and in the Cauca valley, in some of
the neighbouring mountains. To the north of San Agustín lies
the region of Tierradentro, the centre of which is the small town
of Inzá.[25] This sharply dissected and isolated mountain landscape is another important archaeological area which, in some
aspects, seems to be related to San Agustín or, at least, to some
of its developmental phases. In Tierradentro, cist and shaft
graves, carved boulders, statues, and scattered surface sites occur
in many parts, but the local culture is characterized above all by
its huge sepulchral chambers. Cut into the soft rock are large

Fig. 22   underground rooms accessible by steep spiral stairways, the
upper end of which is hidden under earth-covered slabs, no ex-
terior mark indicating the existence of these burial chambers.

Fig. 23   The ground plan is circular or oval, with a series of inset niches
separated by column-like blocks. Square columns chiselled out
of the rock support the roof, which is either vaulted, flat, or cut
on a slant. The inside walls of these chambers, together with
their recesses and columns, are painted in black, white, red, and
yellow, with motifs consisting of parallel lines, lozenges, concentric rhomboids and circles. Large shield-shaped human faces
are painted on the walls, and in some graves there are human
figures carved in relief on the walls and adorned with painted

Fig. 23.   Interior of a rock-cut sepulchral chamber; Tierradentro

designs. Skeletal remains have been found in large urns and shallow pits dug into the floor, and it seems that the aboriginal inhabitants of Tierradentro practised burial by cremation. There are no mounds at Tierradentro, nor have any stone-lined temples or shrines been discovered so far. The statues which are found at several spots – but not in association with the burial chambers – are considerably less stylized or elaborate than those of San Agustín; the faces lack the ferocious expression and are more human. In general terms, Tierradentro stone sculpture represents a less developed phase than its counterpart of the south, but valid comparisons are rather difficult because in both cultures the monolithic stone carvings are highly individualized.

Plate 12

Tierradentro pottery is rather coarse, of a dark brownish colour, and is frequently adorned with snake-like relief bands or triangular human faces. Lines of dots, incised geometric designs, large circles, and coarsely modelled human faces are common modes of decoration. The deep incisions, circles, and dots are often filled with a white paste. Many pottery shapes found at San

Fig. 24

Agustín are also present in Tierradentro, such as tripods, double-spouted vessels, cups with horizontally out-flaring rims, high pedestal bowls, and other forms, decorated in a manner quite similar to the San Agustín varieties. However, the typical Tierradentro ceramics found associated with the painted chamber tombs show little or no resemblance to San Agustín wares.

Most authorities believe that the Tierradentro culture – as represented by the rock-cut chamber tombs – is of a later date than the San Agustín and that the monolithic stone carvings and the painted tombs belong to a late phase of local development. It seems reasonable to suppose that the many different grave types found in both regions reflect not only a social stratification, but also different chronological periods. The rock-cut chambers of Tierradentro may have developed out of simple shaft graves with lateral chambers. Like San Agustín, the Tierradentro region probably contains several long periods

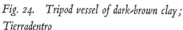

Fig. 24. Tripod vessel of dark-brown clay;
Tierradentro

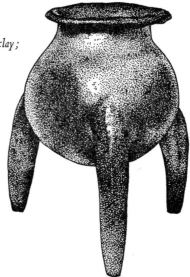

of cultural development and of diverse external influences. To
establish their sequence from detailed pottery analyses is an
important task for the future.[26]

We must turn now to another archaeological area – this time
in the Western Cordillera and the neighbouring Cauca valley.
Due east of the Bay of Buenaventura lie the head-waters of the
Calima river, a large tributary of the lower San Juan. While in
its lower course the Calima crosses the jungle country of the
Chocó rain-forest, its upper course traverses a landscape of rolling
hills, of an entirely different climatic character. At an altitude of
more than 1,000 m. above sea level, the upper Calima drainage
has a pleasant temperate climate and very fertile soils, lying beyond the region of the torrential rainfalls of the Pacific coast.

The Calima river has given its name to an archaeological
area characterized by a certain style of pottery and gold-work,
which, during recent years, has become known mainly through
the activities of treasure-hunters. Very few systematic excava-

tions have been carried out in this region and there is still a lack
of detailed surveys, but the available data suggest that this region
is of major importance in Colombian prehistory.[27] Surface remains in the form of terraced house sites, petroglyphs, and ancient fields are abundant. On the hill-tops and slopes there are
small house platforms, some of them the size of a single dwelling, others of sufficient capacity to accommodate several houses.
Fields with parallel ridges or intersecting ridges forming large
squares, can be observed on many of the higher parts. Most
other archaeological remains known so far come, however,
from looted graves. Characteristic pottery shapes are: sub-

Plates 21-23
globular double-spouted vessels, the divergent spouts being
connected by a flat bridge; anthropomorphic vessels, often representing a crouching figure, the container being a cylindrical
basket carried on the figure's back; vessels with hollow mammiform supports; hemispherical cups with slightly in-turned rims.
Many biomorphic vessels, generally with bulbous supports, represent toads, turtles, birds, and other animals. Decoration consists of finely incised parallel lines, triangles, herring-bone patterns, and lines of dots, or appliqué strips with transverse notches. Red-slipped wares are common and bichrome painting (red
and white) occurs occasionally, as does negative painting. This
pottery corresponds in many details to the one found at the
Catanguero site. The pottery associated with the habitation
sites is far less elaborate and consists mainly of globular vessels
of yellowish or brownish colour, sometimes covered with a red
slip. A rather common type of ware consists of globular vessels
with a short neck and out-flaring rim, provided with three loop
handles, two of them on the upper part of the container and a
third one on the lower part, on the opposite side. Most human
effigies, be they figurines or anthropomorphic containers, show
certain facial features which are of diagnostic interest: the almond-shaped eyes are slanted; the lips are thick, almost Negroid
in shape, and on both sides of the mouth there is a deep vertical

furrow setting off the full cheeks. These are, perhaps, minor details, but they acquire significance for later comparisons.

The burials, generally shaft graves with a vaulted lateral chamber, contain few recognizable skeletal remains, but are rich in elaborate pottery and gold objects. The Calima area is notable for its metallurgy which includes masks, breastplates, diadems, wristlets and necklaces, nose and ear ornaments, and many other finely wrought objects of gold. Trumpets, spoons, and breastplates take very complex forms, combining hollowcast or hammered elements with tubular or discshaped pendants. Stylistically these objects show marked parallels with the San Agustín statuary: the feline features with long, crossed fangs, are characteristic of Calima goldwork; we find *alter ego* representations, and there are many resemblances in the shape of the eyes and mouth. A gold mask of Calima style, but representing a feline deity of San Agustín style, was found at Inzá, in the vicinity of Tierradentro. These resemblances have led many authors to infer a relationship between the two cultures.

Plates 24-26

We shall return to this question shortly, but first we must mention two other cultural areas: Quimbaya and Tumaco. The name 'Quimbaya' has been used indiscriminately for a wide range of prehistoric artifacts of pottery and gold found commonly in the Central Cordillera and the Cauca valley, especially for certain ceramics decorated with negative painting.[28] In reality, the Quimbaya Indians were a historic tribe having, it would seem, little or no connection with the mass of archaeological materials attributed to them. At the time of the Spanish conquest, about 1540, the tribe occupied a relatively small but densely populated territory situated on the western flanks of the Central Cordillera, between the Cauca river and its small eastern tributaries, the Micos and the Guacayca. Although normally a rather pacific tribe, the Quimbaya, under their principal chieftain *Tacurumbí*, put up a fierce resistance against the Spaniards, but were soon overpowered and ceased to exist as a tribal unity early in colonial times. At the time of the conquest, however, the Quimbaya were famous for their elaborate gold, work and the name 'Quimbaya' has been associated ever since with the finely wrought jewellery or the painted pottery found over much of the Central Cordillera and its valleys. Although it is possible to distinguish a certain stylistic unity in the gold objects, which may perhaps be attributed to this tribe, the name 'Quimbaya' should not be applied to the thousands of ceramic vessels which have found their way into many private or mu seum collections, and which have no proven connection – either in space or in time – with the historical Quimbaya. As a matter of fact, the territory where the Spaniards found the Quimbaya had been occupied by this tribe only a short time before the ar rival of the Europeans, their former tribal habitat lying farther north.

The archaeological remains found in this area – not only in Quimbaya territory but in the wider one of the Central Cordil lera – are known mainly from looted tombs, this being tradi tionally one of the richest regions in Colombia for its splendid grave goods. There are many different grave types: shaft graves with side chambers of diverse shapes, sometimes slab lined or provided with steps; pit graves for single or multiple burials; large underground chambers of Tierradentro type; wooden cof fins, and even stone sarcophagi cut out of a single block. Many of these burials are accompanied by large amounts of pottery; the corpse – or corpses – in the different graves are found in various positions: extended, flexed, or disarticulated and reburied in urns. As hardly any systematic excavations have been carried out in this area, the exact associations are unknown and we are able to give only a summary description of a few pottery styles, the precise time position or interrelationships of which are still conjectural.

A quite distinctive ceramic form is the double vessel in which two modelled containers are connected by a cylindrical body

Fig. 25. Zoomorphic vessel; 'Quimbaya' style

and a bridge-like handle. One container is modelled in the shape of an animal, a bird, toad or mammal, while the other one is plain, more or less globular, and is provided with a tubular spout. Sometimes both containers are in the form of animals. Some of these vessels are 'whistling jars' and produce a hissing sound when water is poured from them; many distinctly recall Peruvian ceramics although not of any specific period or region. Another style which is frequent and which we have mentioned already from other regions, is the double-spouted vessel with a loop-shaped handle. In the Central Cordillera the body of this vessel often consists of four lobe-shaped or bulbous mammiform supports, but sub-globular bodies with a dome-shaped upper part, or with a pronounced shoulder, are also frequent. Other common styles are tall pedestal vessels, the upper part forming an open bowl; tall jars with a shouldered conical body and a re-stricted orifice; cylindrical urn-shaped jars with vertical grooves, and a great variety of open bowls: hemispherical, diamond-shaped, with flaring or in-curving sides, or with vertical walls. Square containers, ornamented with deeply excised motifs, are typical of this area. Figurine jars and solid or hollow anthro-

Fig. 25

Plate 13

Plate 17
Fig. 26

Fig. 26. Anthropomorphic vessel; 'Quimbaya' style

pomorphic figurines, are also quite characteristic. The former are large-headed effigies, with spindly extremities, sitting cross-legged or, sometimes, squatting on a low bench. The figurines from the region just south of the Quimbaya proper, are often slab-shaped and square in outline, while toward the north they are somewhat less stylized and have rounded heads and more realistic features. Boat-shaped vessels made of a dark-brown, brittle clay, are found at many sites. Decoration ranges from incising, tubular stamping, and painting, to excision, appliqué ridges, and modelling. Positive painting in red, white, black, and yellow is common and two- or three-colour negative painting is very characteristic. Many vessels bear a fine red slip but there are also finely polished black and brown wares.

Plates 15-16

Fig. 27

Fig. 28

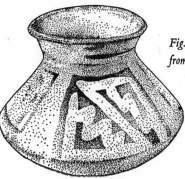

Fig. 27. Painted vessel of 'Quimbaya' style from the Nariño area

104

Fig. 29

Fig. 28. Painted pottery of 'Quimbaya' style

Other artifacts besides pottery are frequently found in graves, such as flat rectangular, bar-shaped, cylindrical, or tubular stamps. Many of these stamps bear intricate positive designs cut deeply into the surface, and one can imagine the splendid decorations thus produced on the body or on cotton cloth. Clay spindle whorls, of conical, double-conical, or disk shape, are often covered with finely incised or punched designs, filled with a white paste. Finely polished obsidian mirrors, with a convex

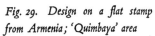

Fig. 29. Design on a flat stamp from Armenia; 'Quimbaya' area

Fig. 30. Design on a cylindrical clay stamp; 'Quimbaya' area

Fig. 31. Bar-shaped clay stamp; 'Quimbaya' area

back, have been found in some graves, and also polished stone celts, necklace beads of polished rock crystal or quartzite, and many other small artifacts of clay and stone. The grave-looters are also said to have found wooden paddles, cotton cloth, and weapons of a hard palm wood.

A glance at any collection of so-called 'Quimbaya' pottery shows that there are conspicuous stylistic and technological differences, probably expressing not only regional variations but differences in chronology and cultural tradition. Some of this pottery may be Quimbaya, but much of it belongs to different periods, the exact content and time-sequence of which has not yet been established. It is a pity indeed that this most important area of Colombia has been left almost entirely to the devastating activities of treasure-hunters.

The metallurgy of the Central Cordillera was highly developed and as the chroniclers speak of the gold-work of the Quimbaya and their neighbours, we can correlate some of the archaeological specimens with this historical tribe. The 'Quimbaya' style is characterized by finely cast objects of pure gold, but *tumbaga,* a mixture of gold and copper, was also frequently used and in some regions copper objects such as bells, disks, and wire are

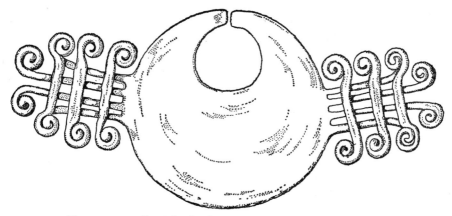

Fig. 32.   Gold nose ornament of 'Quimbaya' style

quite common. Metallurgical techniques show a notable ad‐
vance over the Calima gold‐work. There is some hammered
gold, but we find abundant evidence for melting, forging, and
soldering as well. Hollow or open casting in the *cire‐perdue* tech‐ Plates 31, 32
nique is the most distinctive feature. The objects manufactured
by the aboriginal goldsmiths include breast‐plates, masks, scep‐
tres, bracelets, nose or ear ornaments, and a large variety of bio‐
morphic pendants, often in the shape of fantastic animals.
Among the finest pieces are gold vessels and bottles, and large
anthropomorphic figurines. Fish‐hooks, tweezers, and needles
are also frequent.[29]

It seems that, at an unknown date, the Cauca cultures of Ca‐
lima and 'Quimbaya' type extended as far east as the banks of
the Magdalena river. In the region of El Guamo, near the con‐
fluence of the Saldaña river with the Magdalena, some inter‐
esting finds have been made which point in this direction. A
number of deep shaft graves, belonging probably to different
periods, were found to contain grave goods which can be
clearly correlated with the Cauca valley. One group of shaft
graves with lateral chambers contained the following ceramics: a
typical Calima vessel representing a toad with bulbous legs, pro‐

Fig. 33.   A lizard of gold; 'Quimbaya' style

Fig. 34

vided with a vertical tubular spout and a loop handle; several globular and sub-globular vessels with narrow necks, decorated with scrolls, spirals, and lozenge-shaped elements painted in red on a cream background. While these vessels undoubtedly show Cauca affiliations, another type points rather to the Peruvian coast. This type consists of massive containers of sub-globular shape; on the dome-like upper part there are two vertical tubular spouts, connected by a flat bridge. The upper part of these heavy vessels is decorated with deep indentations. The lower half is formed of ten or twelve large modelled lobes, perhaps meant to represent a fruit.

Another cemetery shows a different type of grave. The tombs consist of square pits, 2 m. deep, on the floor of which the corpse was buried in an extended position. The entire pit was filled with layers of heavy, rounded stones taken from the near-by river. Close to the head of one of the corpses a single pottery vessel was found, a sub-globular container resting on a flat pedestal base. Modelled on the upper part of the container is a square house, the gable roof being supported by four posts on each side. A tubular spout opens through the ridge of the

Fig. 35

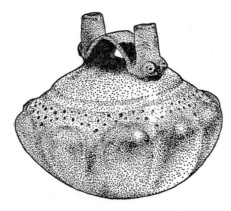

*Fig. 34. Double-spouted vessel
from El Guamo; Tolima district*

Fig. 35. Vessel in the shape of a house; El Guamo, Tolima district

roof. The vessel has a red slip and is covered with traces of spiral designs in red paint. A neighbouring grave of similar type contained a large oval nose ornament of gold, of a type common in the Calima-'Quimbaya' areas. At Ríoblanco, on the headwaters of the Saldaña river, a number of gold and pottery objects have been found which also point to close affinities with the aforementioned cultures.

The four archaeological cultures, or rather culture-provinces, we have described in these pages – San Agustín, Tierradentro, Calima, and 'Quimbaya' – represent some of the highest developments in western Colombia and, although they differ from one another in many aspects, they share a number of significant features. All of them are based on intensive maize farming and sedentary village life; ancient fields with ridges and furrows are common to all of them; a well defined social order is suggested by the discriminative treatment of the dead; burial rites point to an emphasis on ceremonial. The pottery has the following traits in common: double-spouted bridged vessels, multiple bulbous supports, pedestal bases, negative painting, finely decorated spindle whorls, and anthropomorphic vessels or figurines. Stone carvings are found in all four areas, and the metallurgy of gold and copper also links these regions together. Calima gold-work shows stylistic relationships with San Agustín and, technologically and stylistically, many Calima and so-called 'Quimbaya' ceramics are quite similar. There is a relationship between San Agustín and Tierradentro, and the painted sepulchral chambers of the latter area are found also in other regions of the Cauca valley, extending towards the south at least as far as Pasto.

At the beginning of this chapter we referred to the foreign influences intruding on the Pacific coast. It was there, about 500 BC, that a new cultural influx, coming from the outside, in all probability from Mesoamerica, had made itself felt. We are not suggesting here that the higher cultures of the Cauca valley and the neighbouring mountain regions arose simultaneously from a common source, but rather that the local cultures received, at different times and in varying intensities, a lasting impulse from Mesoamerican settlers who contributed in a high degree to the subsequent cultural pattern of the Sub-Andean chiefdoms. We have already mentioned that this influence can be traced from the San Juan river southward, increasing toward the Tumaco area and continuing into Ecuador, and we shall shortly refer to this part of the coast in greater detail. But before turning to this area the following observations are pertinent. In recent years evidence has been accumulating that the Chavín horizon of Peru is not a local development of the Central Andean cultures, but that its roots are derived from a Mesoamerican source located in the Olmec country. Mesoamerican navigators coasting along the shores of the Pacific apparently introduced into Peru the jaguar cult and many elements of the associated art style, together with maize farming. This contact dates from the ninth century BC or even earlier and it seems probable that it was then that the idea of the jaguar cult was also introduced into Colombia by Mesoamerican travellers, colonists and cultists who first established themselves on the Pacific coast and then, retreating from the unfavourable climate, penetrated toward the east, into regions where the agricultural potential for maize cultivation was more propitious. The roots of San Agustín culture may well go back to this time-level, and if San Agustín shows also certain features which have their parallels in Central America, these may have their origins in later contacts and later colonies of Meso- and Central American settlers. On the other hand, the diffusion was not a one-way process, from north to south only, as it is also evident that Peruvian elements were introduced into Colombia by the same routes.

But now we must turn to the evidence for a second stage of Mesoamerican influences, which we have dated at about 500 BC. The island of Tumaco, and the neighbouring shores and river banks, have recently become known for the many elaborate clay artifacts of Mesoamerican type, found eroded on the beaches or buried in mounds, locally called *tolas*.[30] This pottery which has been given the name Tumaco culture, does not form a single, easily defined complex, but consists of elements of many different periods. The most characteristic forms are anthropomorphic figurines, many of them small but others reaching a height of more than 30 cm. These effigies are technically and aesthetically among the finest ceramics of aboriginal America and include a wide range of human representations: men or women, generally standing; people wearing masks, warriors with high elaborate feather head-dresses, a mother carrying an infant in her lap, all of them showing many details of dress and ornament such as skirts, aprons and loin-cloths, necklaces, ear

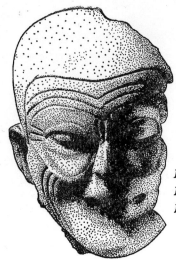

Fig. 36.   Clay mask; Tumaco area
Fig. 37.   Head of a clay figurine; Tumaco area
Fig. 38.   Head of a bearded figurine; Tumaco area

plugs, and many other elements. Some of the figurines show a marked occipito-frontal head deformation. Animal effigies represent jaguars and reptiles, owls, snakes, and snarling dragon-like monsters with long fangs and protruding tongues. Some-

Plates 27–30

times the head of an animal or monster is combined with a human body and in other representations a human face peers through the diamond-shaped wide-open beak or mouth of a monstrous owl-like bird or a jaguar. A headless figurine has its head placed inside the body whence it looks out through a tri-angular 'window'. Some of the heads are highly individualized and seem to be almost portraits of specific persons. Some show

Fig. 36

old men, occasionally bearded, with wrinkled faces and tooth-less mouths. A concept of dualism is frequently shown by splitting the face vertically into two halves with different expres-sions, at times showing half a skull and half a living person. Many of the figurines are mould-made and whole moulds or fragments of them have occasionally been found.

Among pottery shapes, one of the most frequent is that of the double-spouted vessel with bridge handle, the globular

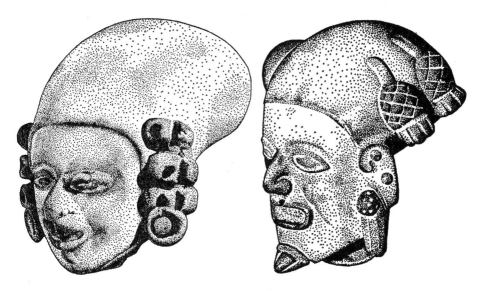

container being topped by a hemispherical bulge from which protrude the divergent tubular spouts. Globular vessels with annular bases, short necks and out-flaring rims often have a peripherical flange or ridge. Cups in the shape of a jaguar's or tapir's foot have been found at several sites and small ladles, with handles in the shape of a human penis, occur from time to time. The main decorative techniques are modelling, appliqué elements, and incision, but some of the pottery and the figurines bear painted designs, sometimes in a negative technique, some-times in a striking blue colour which was applied after the ob-ject had been fired.

We cannot here embark on detailed stylistic comparisons with other cultures; suffice it to say that the Tumaco culture and its different phases are undoubtedly of Mesoamerican origin. The exact points of origin, however, seem to have changed through time and while some traits point to the Mexican Gulf area, other suggest Oaxaca and the Pacific coast, the central highlands of Mexico, the Maya area, and also some of the Central American cultures of Costa Rica and Nicaragua. The

Fig. 37

Fig. 41

overseas contacts between Mesoamerica and the Pacific coast of
Colombia were certainly not limited to casual visits but were
mainly due to settlers who colonized the coast at several spots
and at different periods. On the other hand, some of the features
observed in Tumaco point to contacts with the Peruvian coast,
but in this case, too, the points of origin and the time-period
change and make it difficult to follow this diffusion in detail.

A large mound of more than 3 m. of refuse accumulation has
been excavated on the Mataje river and produced evidence for
a sequence of at least three phases, and excavations on several
other rivers and beaches of the vicinity have added a copious
body of ceramic and lithic materials. The oldest radiocarbon
date for the Mataje sequence places the end of Period I at 400
BC. A date of 300 BC marks the beginning of Period II and
this lasts – through a sequence of minor phases – until AD 10,
when it is followed by Period III materials. Among the oldest
pottery types we find again double-spouted vessels with bridge
handles,[31] tall tripods, and bowls with bulbous mammiform
supports. It is here, then, on this time-level and in this area, that
we find the origin of the same ceramic types in the Cauca valley,
the Andean core-land, and the Central Cordillera. Period II
of the Mataje mound, dated to about 300 BC, corresponds in
detail to Catanguero, the site on the lower Calima river and
which has a radiocarbon date of 250 BC. This site, it will be
recalled, produced pottery related to the elaborate wares found
in the Calima area, and Period II contains figurines with the
same thick-lipped features and deep vertical furrows on both
sides of the mouth as are typical of the Calima region. We can
thus follow the intrusion of Mesoamerican influences into the
Cauca valley where, once they had left behind the inhospitable
coastal regions, they profoundly influenced the local Colombian cultures and, indeed provided the inspiration for their
higher development.[32] The entire shaft tomb-figurine complex
of the Cauca Valley and the Central Cordillera may well be

derived from Western Mexico (Nayarit-Jalisco-Colima), where radiocarbon dates of approximately AD 250 have been obtained for a late phase of chamber tombs and anthropo-morphic figurines.

We must summarize at this point and draw some tentative conclusions. It seems that Mesoamerican influences in Colom-bia date from as early as about 1200 BC, when such elements as the jaguar cult, maize cultivation, burial mounds, monolithic sarcophagi, and obsidian mirrors were introduced by sporadic settlers who penetrated from the Pacific coast toward the east. About 500 BC, a second period of major Mesoamerican influ-ences began, bringing in its wake such elements as deep-level shaft graves with lateral chambers, elaborate figurines, occipito-frontal head deformation, pottery with multiple supports, perhaps double-spouted vessels, flat and cylindrical stamps, elaborate spindle whorls, and biomorphic whistles. Both periods of influence gave rise to a new culture pattern which has been designated the Sub-Andean stage and which can briefly be characterized thus: seed agriculture provided the principal foundation for sedentary village life and, although shifting agriculture continued, settlements were now far more permanent than during the previous stage. The consequent concentration of an increasing population led to social stratification, craft specialization and high technological development and trade. Wider political cohesion was achieved only in those instances where a group of neighbouring valleys became united under a powerful local chief. Religious practices centred around a priest-temple-idol complex, including a jaguar cult, artificial mounds, and large cemeteries, while shamanistic practices employed small human figurines of diverse types. It is possible that human sacrifice and head trophies were also introduced from Meso-america at one of the major periods of contact.

It is interesting to examine for a moment the culture of the Cauca tribes and chiefdoms of the sixteenth century, for Mesoamerican elements. For some of the groups of the 'Quimbaya' area the chroniclers report the following characteristics: warfare for the purpose of securing sacrifical victims; the privileged status of the victim; sacrifice on a high platform structure accessible by a stair flanked by idols; heart removal; flayed-skin trophies; exhibition of trophy skulls. To this, undoubtedly Mesoameri-can, complex we may add occipito-frontal head deformation, dental mutilations, and systematic bee-keeping.

CHAPTER VII

The Lowland Chiefdoms and their Neighbours

URING THE FIRST MILLENNIUM BC, important
developments took place in many parts of the coastal and
inter-Andean lowlands. In most regions intensive maize farming provided the economic basis for the spread of settlements,
but not all of them achieved the permanency or technological
level characteristic of the Sub-Andean cultures. Some of the
dwellings were grouped into compact villages but others were
scattered and remained on a Formative level. In some regions
there was a marked return to the riverine environment, in part
by groups unable, perhaps, to compete with the more integrated
societies which had carved out for themselves little chiefdoms
and had taken firm possession of the fertile slopes; in part because trade relationships were becoming increasingly important
and for these the rivers offered the best means of communica-
tion. Gold, cotton cloth, salt, and other articles were traded now
over large distances and, in consequence, the riparian communities were becoming somewhat more 'cosmopolitan' and open
to new influences, than the groups which lived in the more
isolated mountain valleys of the interior.

Let us consider first the Caribbean lowlands and the developments which followed upon Momil. In the valley of the Ranchería river, a wide depression lying between the Sierra Nevada
and the northernmost range of the Eastern Cordillera, we find a
sequence of local cultures which are known by the names of
their type-sites: La Loma-El Horno-Los Cocos-Portacelli.[33]
The sites, most of them deep middens with dense accumulations of occupational refuse, are located on the river banks and
on small streams, and the heavy *metates* indicate the presence of
sedentary maize farmers. Manioc may have been of some importance in their economy, for there are many fragments of large

clay platters. Today this is a very arid region forming part of the wider Guajira landscape, but in times past there must have been higher rainfall and different types of vegetation and fauna. Some sites lie on the periphery of depressions which seem to have been lagoons or swamps; others are on the banks of dry stream-beds and gullies which today, even during the rainy season, carry hardly a trickle of water. Faunal remains such as mammal bones and certain snails belong to species we associate with a damp forest environment, and the aquatic birds so frequently depicted on some of the pottery have long since disappeared from this region.

The Loma-Horno periods constitute the so-called 'First Painted Horizon' in this part of the country, characterized by

Fig. 39. Polychrome designs on pottery from El Horno, Ranchería river

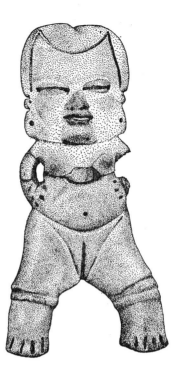

Fig. 40. Anthropomorphic figurine from El Horno, Rancheria river

the predominant use of bichrome and polychrome painting. Curvilinear elements are typical: spirals, wavy lines, sigmoid patterns, or comb-like designs, painted in red and black on a finely-slipped cream-coloured background. There is an abun- dance of vessel shapes: flat dishes, pedestal cups, composite- silhouette vessels, and small bowls with multiple supports. A brilliant black ware has incised curvilinear decoration, often with a white pigment fill added to make the designs stand out against the dark background. Hollow anthropomorphic clay figurines with bulbous legs and naturalistic features are fre- quent in the El Horno period and are often painted in bright colours. The two periods show an emphasis on modelled and colourful ceramics, in contrast to the former incised tradition. With the Los Cocos period bichrome painting (black or red on white) begins to predominate, together with rectilinear designs,

Fig. 39

Fig. 40

and this new development has been named the 'Second Painted Horizon'. Cylindrical urns with modelled and painted human faces on the walls, contain the remains of secondary burials and there is evidence for cremation. The Portacelli period continues, in many ways, this bichrome-geometric tradition. Characteristic pottery types are corrugated vessels, in which the coils used in the vessel's construction are left on the outside, and beautifully finished cups of fine, red-slipped clay, covered with bird designs in black. The figurines of this period are stiffer, standing on straight cylindrical legs, and are much more stylized than the earlier ones. Several extended burials have been found, the skull resting on a large open dish.

Fig. 41

In north-eastern Colombia, the four periods of the Ranchería sequence extend from the mouth of that river to the valley of the Cesar river, and cover the lower parts of the neighbouring Sierra Nevada. In the Eastern Cordillera El Horno pottery has been found near Bochalema, on the head-waters of the Zulia river which flows into the Gulf of Maracaibo. A painted pottery complex of the head-waters of the Chicamocha river, some 150 km. south of Bochalema, also shows traces of El Horno ancestry. This part of the Eastern Cordillera is, archaeologically speaking, quite unexplored but stray finds of painted pottery point to relationships with the Ranchería valley. In western Venezuela the Ranchería cultures are represented by a series of very similar complexes which range from the end of the first millennium BC (e.g., La Pitía, Tocuyano) to protohistoric times (e.g., Dabajuro, Tierra de los Indios).[34] The antecedents of our two painted horizons seem to lie outside of Colombian territory. The polychrome wares of La Loma and El Horno are probably in part derived from Momil, but there are very strong resemblances with the polychrome pottery of Panama, especially with the Coclé complex. Although there is some evidence for a west-to-east overland diffusion, from Panama across northern Colombia to western Venezuela, the possibility of diffusion by

Fig. 41.   Black on red designs from Portacelli, Rancheria river

coastal navigation cannot be disregarded. Pottery with curvilinear polychrome decoration, and solid anthropomorphic figurines, are found at several sites near Bonda and Mamatoco, a
short distance inland from the Bay of Santa Marta, and stray
finds from the lower Magdalena also suggest an inland penetration originating on the coast. Such contacts probably did not
take place at any one specific period, but may have taken the
form of various immigrant movements, by which these pottery
traditions reached Colombia and Venezuela, from lower Central America.

The Portacelli folk seem to have abandoned their habitat on
the Rancheria river in protohistoric times, perhaps under the
pressure of progressive dessication. The rise of the Tairona culture (see Chapter VIII) in the neighbouring Sierra Nevada
may have been a contributing factor leading to the drying-up
of streams whose head-waters were deforested by the slash-and-
burn technique of their agriculture. Only isolated groups of
Portacelli Indians survived till the arrival of the Europeans in

the foot-hills of the Sierra Nevada, notably in the valleys of Río Seco and Badillo, where the typical red-slipped cups with bird designs have been found in pit graves associated with iron trade axes; but by that time their colourful pottery had greatly declin-ed in craftsmanship and the compact villages had been split up into scattered homesteads in the mountain folds.

Fig. 42

On the lower Magdalena river, a centre of major importance was the region of Zambrano. We have mentioned this place earlier when speaking of the first inland movements of the ar-chaic shell-mound dwellers and their fibre-tempered pottery, and now we find here an almost uninterrupted record of aboriginal settlement through nearly four thousand years. Today Zam-brano is a small village of Creole peasants and cattle-breeders, but in prehistoric times this was a most important contact area where influences converged from many different directions: from the coast, the Sierra Nevada, the Sinú valley, the tribes

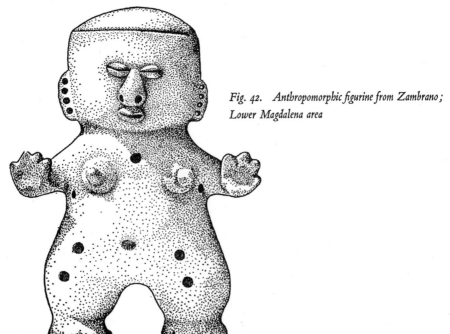

Fig. 42. Anthropomorphic figurine from Zambrano; Lower Magdalena area

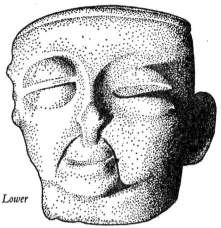

Fig. 43. Head of a clay figurine from Zambrano; Lower Magdalena area

living up-river, and many others. Of the more than fifty sites investigated in this region, some are representative of the Puerto Hormiga, Momil, and Malambo phases, some are like those of the decentralized maize farmers, whilst theirs, again, resemble the large riverine villages of the early Sub-Andean stage. By the middle of the seventh century AD, we find here on the flat river bank a settlement pattern of large mounds serving as house platforms, built partly of heaped-up earth and partly of thick midden deposits. Some of these sites show a depth of 6 m. of potsherds and stone objects. A few centuries later compact villages with large cemeteries of urn burials appear. Necklace beads of carnelian from the Sierra Nevada, gold pieces from the Sinú, and objects made from sea-shells, bear witness to far-flung trade relations. The pottery of these later phases, beginning at the time of the house platforms or perhaps earlier, is extremely well made, with an abundance of well-defined styles: cups, plates and dishes, pedestal bowls with thin cylindrical bases, anthropomorphic vessels, animal effigies, spindle whorls, all decorated with finely incised geometric motifs or with appliqué pellets or strips. A shiny black ware is also common. Some of the earlier phases of Zambrano possess features which may provide the key to the question of why this region became a centre

Plates 45, 46

Plates 38, 39

123

of importance in the midst of the small farming and fishing communities of the Magdalena flood-plains. Several anthropo-morphic vessels and figurines bear a striking resemblance to Calima ware, especially in such details as the puffy cheeks and the deep vertical furrows at the side of the mouth.

Different phases of the long sequence found at Zambrano can be observed at many places along the lower Magdalena.[35] In the vicinity of the lagoon of Zapatosa, at the confluence of the Cesar and Magdalena rivers, are still to be found the remains of small villages whose inhabitants combined farming with fishing. The many hundreds of stone celts found in some of these sites point to the manufacture of dug-out canoes, and even today this part of the lower Magdalena is still famous for its well-made dug-outs, the shape of which seems to have changed very little since prehistoric times. Across the river and south of the lagoon of Zapatosa the slopes of Cerro Barco and the foot-hills of the Serranía de San Lucas are covered with many hundreds of small house sites consisting of circular or semicircular house platforms, partly dug into the mountainside, partly built up of earth, often with an encircling ring of irregular stones. Between the scattered houses there are small agricultural terraces with retaining walls of stones set close together, to avoid soil erosion. The same settlement pattern can be observed to the south-west, on the head-waters of the Nechí river, and in the hills of Tubará, Piojó, Luruaco, and other places between Barranquilla and Cartagena.[36] These rudimentary architectural features are hard-ly more than an occasional adaptation to the broken terrain, and they are not accompanied by a higher cultural development in other respects. Most of the lowland communities remained on an essentially Formative level of small village farmers, with no wider political cohesion, nor any marked social or religious complexity. They formed small local chiefdoms, trading with each other and at times, perhaps, warring with each other, but never achieving a political unity beyond the narrow confines of their own lagoons, their own range of hills, or their own stretch of river.

This pattern changes very little as we move west, toward the San Jorge and Sinú rivers. On the upper Sinú, the Tierra Alta phase has been defined; this derives from the maize farming communities which combined agriculture with fishing.[37] Deeply hollowed bedrock mortars for seed grinding, and an abundance of netsinkers made from notched stone disks, suggest such an economic basis, and the deep midden accumulations around the house sites point to permanency of settlement. The pottery is competent but rather drab. Next to the usual globular and sub/globular culinary pots there are cups with annular bases and horizontally out/flaring rims, small bowls with multiple supports, flat/bottomed bowls and deep dishes, and some an/ thropomorphic vessels. Grater/bowls, open containers with the inside roughened by deeply incised lines, may have been used for grinding chili peppers or other condiments. Decorative techniques include, characteristically, zoned punctation, appli/ qué strips and pellets, flat triangular impressions produced with a pointed tool, coarse incised lines in a herring/bone pattern, but no painting and very little modelling. Small sites with simi/ lar cultural contents are found at many spots along the Sinú river and in the neighbouring hills, and extend north/eastward toward Cartagena and south/westward toward the Gulf of Urabá.

On the middle course of the Sinú and also on the San Jorge river, we find the remains of a culture which advanced consider/ ably more and which represents a truly Sub/Andean level. The type/sites are the lagoon of Betancí (Sinú) and the Caño Viloria (San Jorge) respectively, but this complex covers a wide area between the two rivers. The Betancí/Viloria complex is characterized by large burial mounds and house platforms, which can be easily located on the grassy flood/plain. One of the principal mounds at Betancí has an oval ground plan meas/

uring 60 by 40 m., and is more than 8 m. high. This is probably the largest earthwork known so far from Colombia. At a
distance varying between 70 to 100 m. from the foot of the
mound, a low ridge, 13 m. wide and rather more than one
metre high, encircles the entire structure. Unfortunately, treasure hunters have perforated the mound in all directions but
stray sherds from their diggings prove that this structure belongs
to the BetancíViloria complex as defined in controlled excavations nearby. The excavation of several smaller mounds in the
vicinity shows that these had been built over one or more extended burials accompanied by grave goods in the form of pottery, and objects of gold, copper, and shell. The same ceramic
types were observed in the house platforms, both on the Sinú
and San Jorge rivers. The pottery of this complex is quite different from that described so far from other regions of the coastal
lowlands. A characteristic type consists of a high pedestal cup
(up to 70 cm. tall), of reddish sandtempered clay. The
relatively small hemispherical or dishshaped container rests on
Plate 42 a large hollow base shaped like an elongated bell, the outside of
which is decorated with several female figures modelled in clay
and standing with their backs against it. These figures are in fact
sculptures which were modelled apart, in the round, and then
stuck to the vessel's wall. Similar figurines are also found adorning the walls of large globular vessels with flat bases and short
necks. The realistically sculptured figures show smiling women
clad only in short skirts, the upper part of their bodies covered
with intricate incised designs probably representing tattooing or
paint. Occasionally there are also freestanding figurines which
do not form part of a container. A dark burnished ware is deco
Plate 43 rated with deeply excised designs of meanders, rhomboid elements, crosses, etc. It takes the shape of pedestal bowls with
high tubular bases, subglobular vessels with annular supports,
and several types of composite silhouette vessels. Shoeshaped
vessels are also found. Another characteristic style consists of

globular pots of different sizes, decorated with black and red Plate 40
painted designs on a cream background. Open bowls with
annular bases are decorated with incised lines and there are large
grater-bowls and simple hemispherical bowls of various sizes. Plate 41
A large realistic figurine representing a man sitting on a four-
legged bench and holding a staff in his hands, comes from the
San Jorge river. Disk-shaped spindle whorls of clay, decorated
with incised patterns, and bar-shaped stamps are also among
the grave goods or are found in the midden deposits. Gold objects include nose and ear ornaments, pendants, animal effigies
on staff heads, and a great many other pieces. Hollow-cast twin-
figurines of birds, reptiles, or fantastic animals are typical. Shell
ornaments are much in evidence and consist of necklace beads
or pendants in the form of birds, frogs, or thin bars, whilst polished cone-shaped objects of shell, provided with suspension
holes, were used as penis coverings.

It is evident that here we have a new culture which has no
local precedents in the coastal lowlands and which must have
penetrated from the south, probably from the Cauca valley. The
physical type depicted on the figurines and anthropomorphic
vessels, the excised decoration, the spindle whorls, the bar-
shaped stamps, and also the gold-work show close similarities
with the so-called Quimbaya area and the regions lying north
of it, in the mountains of the district of Antioquia.

The Betancí-Viloria complex shows a number of characteristics that are associated with the Sub-Andean stage. Maize cultivation on the fertile flood-plains, together with trade, furnished
a stable economic basis, and agricultural techniques were sufficiently advanced to cope with the problem of periodic flooding.
In many parts of the San Jorge valley one can still observe hundreds of acres covered with parallel ridges separated by furrows,
providing well-drained fields for maize and other crops. Differ-
entiation in the treatment of the dead indicates a hierarchical
society and the large ceremonial or agricultural earthworks point

to an organized labour force. The pottery, together with the gold and shell objects, suggest craft specialization and the religious structure seems to have developed far beyond the level of mere shamanistic practices. The extraordinary wealth with which some of the dead were buried suggests the presence of chiefs and priests of considerable power and prestige.

The culture represented by these mound-builders and gold-smiths was still flourishing when the first Spanish expeditions entered the Sinú valley, about 1530. According to early sources, the entire region was divided into three 'Sinú' (or Senú, Cenú) countries: *Fincenú*, including the present Sinú valley; *Pancenú*, corresponding to the San Jorge drainage; and *Cenúfana*, occu-pying the valley of the Nechí river. The chieftains of these three divisions or tribal confederations were brothers who, in their persons, combined political authority with priestly functions, A large temple is described, holding as many as 1,000 people. There were 24 large wooden idols covered with gold, and near the temple rose burial mounds of chiefs or other leaders, each one marked by a tree on which hung a golden bell. There are indications that religious practices centred on a jaguar cult. It is no wonder that the golden treasures of the Sinú led to the rapid extermination of the Indians and the thorough looting of the burial mounds. Today this area is Colombia's main cattle-breeding country. When high ground is sought, corrals and salt-licks are sometimes built on the top of ancient mounds and it still happens that the hooves of the gathering cattle turn up gold nose-rings and finely-cast bird effigies.

On the beaches and off-shore islands between the mouth of the Magdalena and the Gulf of Urabá, a simple farmer-fisher folk had meanwhile established a number of small villages and camp-sites, many of them on barren sand-hills. The material culture known from these sites has been named the Crespo complex, after the type-site near Cartagena.[38] Evidence of occupation is provided by middens and urn-burials, the

Fig. 44. Flat clay stamp from the Gulf of Urabá

latter consisting of cylindrical vessels covered with a few large sherds. Other pottery shapes include griddles, grater-bowls, cups and dishes with annular bases, and globular water containers with constricted necks. Decoration takes the form of simple incised designs and dotted areas. Some vessels are decorated with round human faces and a few figurines have been found in the middens. Very characteristic of the Crespo complex are the many celts and axes made of large sea-shells (*Strombus gigas*) and which had probably been used in the manufacture of dug-out canoes. Large grinding stones and *manos* point to maize farming. Farther inland the Crespo complex has been found on the low hills bordering the coast. There are typological relationships with late Zambrano materials and it seems that Crespo developed out of the Momil-Malambo traditions, as a late local adaptation to the littoral environment. The type-site has been carbon-dated to the late thirteenth century AD and the distribution-pattern of the middens corresponds to that of fisher-folk and maize farmers the Spaniards found established in this area about a century later.

Plates 44, 47

Fig. 44

We must turn now to an entirely different area: the Pacific Lowlands. In this part of tropical Colombia aboriginal cultural developments took a very different course. Except in the

extreme south where the climate and the soils were more propitious, the level of culture did not advance beyond small forest-
dwelling communities which frequently changed their house
sites. In the rain-forest region of the San Juan river we find a
fairly dense prehistoric occupation by the early ninth century
AD, consisting of small agricultural settlements on the banks of
the main river and some of its tributaries. The Murillo complex,
as this culture has been called, is characterized by a brownish,
sand-tempered ware which is found in midden sites associated
with lithic artifacts. Vessel shapes are mainly globular or sub-
globular cooking pots, without handles or supports, with a
large orifice and a simple out-flaring rim. Some of these vessels
are decorated with deeply incised straight lines, forming meander patterns, concentric squares, or groups of parallel lines or
rows of dashes. The lithic material consists of T-shaped axes,
with lateral projections for tying them to a handle, and a variety
of scraping tools and hammer-stones. Grinding slabs and *manos*
are absent, and the economy seems to have been based on root-
crops and the gathering of palm fruits, hunting and fishing.
Radiocarbon tests show this complex to date from about AD
800–900 by which time a new cultural tradition appears, the
Minguimalo complex. The Minguimalo folk were maize farmers using large *metates* and their culture expanded rapidly over
the San Juan drainage and the neighbouring rivers. The pottery is a drab brownish colour, with simple globular shapes, but
the decorative techniques are highly characteristic. One type is
decorated with rows of knobs, or rather, bubbles, produced by
pushing a thin stick against the inner surface of the vessel until
it produces a raised 'bubble' on the outside. The stick is then
withdrawn and the little orifice it leaves is smeared over with
clay, so that the bosses appearing on the outside of the vessel
wall are hollow. Another mode of decoration consists of finger-
nail impressions forming rows of little crescent-shaped imprints.
Sometimes the whole finger-tip is impressed in the soft clay and

in this manner rows of dots or incisions are produced which cover the neck and the upper part of the containers. The celts and axes associated with this pottery are of simple trapezoidal form and lack the lateral projections that characterize the Murillo complex. Nothing is known of the origins of these two complexes neither of which seem to have local antecedents in the Chocó area. We can only note here that finger-nail impressions as a decorative device are found in some prehistoric pottery complexes of the upper Amazon area.

In the Bay of Cupica, on the northern part of the Pacific coast, a large burial mound has been excavated which contained 38 secondary burials accompanied by many pottery vessels, a few spindle whorls, a small gold nose ornament, and several stone artifacts.[40] The burials had been made at different periods and four main phases have been recognized: three of superimposed burials and at least one consisting of an artificial fill which contained midden materials. The pottery of the oldest burials is of a reddish or grayish colour and the sub-globular vessels – most of them simple culinary wares – often show a sharp shoulder. The coarse uneven surfaces are decorated with irregular parallel incised lines and rows of dots; dentate stamping was produced with the edge of a shell and occurs on several specimens. The middle phase contains red-ware culinary vessels of sub-globular or globular shape. The decoration is zoned-incised, showing meander patterns, rows of dots, and areas painted dull red. The interior of the rims is often painted a bright red colour, and many vessels have a red slip. The uppermost layer of burials contains pottery of many different shapes and decorative techniques. Bottle-shaped containers and tall pedestal cups are characteristic, and the bodies of many vessels show large bosses at the shoulder produced by applying pressure from the inside. Incised and modelled decoration is frequent, and some vessels are decorated with polychrome painting and modelled zoomorphic figures.

The associations of the Cupica sequence seem to be various. The earliest pottery, decorated with dentate stamping, shows certain similarities with Momil and with Ciénaga de Oro, a complex closely related to Momil. The later phases contain parallels with Tierra Alta and Betancí. It seems then that the cultures of Cupica were related to those of the Sinú valley. On the other hand, some of the Cupica wares are closely related to Panamanian ceramics from the Madden Lake area and from Coclé. Several vessels of the late phase of Cupica correspond to late Coclé styles, e.g. 'Panelled Red' and 'Early Smoked Ware'. There are evident affinities, too, with archaeological materials found on the Pearl Islands, off the coast of Panama. All this suggests a late penetration from the Pacific coast of Panama, undoubtedly by sea, which established small colonies on the Colombian beaches and eventually reached the area of Bahía Solano where stray finds of the same pottery types bear witness to this southward advance. A radiocarbon date of AD 1227, for the latest burials of Cupica, corresponds to Late Coclé in Panama.

In other parts of the Pacific coast, on the beaches and inlets, and in the mangrove swamps south of Buenaventura, there are small house and midden sites mainly containing ceramics of late type, sometimes related to the San Juan river complexes, sometimes to late Tumaco styles. Proceeding toward the south, approximately from the Guapi river onward, Tumaco influence increases and there are many sites which are related to the different phases of the Mataje sequence. Some of these sites are quite late; a large midden accumulation at Imbilí, on the Mira river, dates from about AD 1000. Ascending some of the rivers toward the crest of the Western Cordillera, we soon find cultures related to the painted complexes of the Cauca valley. On the head-waters of the Patía river a number of deep shaft graves have been excavated, containing single or multiple extended burials. A curious feature of these is that the entrance to the lateral chamber is closed with a large globular jar, the orifice of which is orientated toward the corpse, while the bottom points toward the shaft of the grave. Globular or sub-globular vessels decorated with very complex geometric designs painted in red and black were found among the grave goods, together with small objects of gold or *tumbaga*, and clay spindle whorls.

Similar shaft graves with side chambers are frequent in the southern part of the Colombian Andes, in the direction of Ecuador, and continue from there toward the north and the Cauca valley. On the Hacienda La Marquesa near Popayán, on the head-waters of the Cauca, was discovered a shaft grave which yielded an extraordinary collection of grave goods.[42] Several large anthropomorphic figurines of clay show warriors holding round shields and wearing crested head-dresses. The squat bodies sit on low, four-legged benches. On the back of the figures a crested animal is shown in a climbing position, recalling an *alter ego* representation. The calves of the figurine's legs are swollen and deformed by tight ligatures applied below the knee and above the ankle, a feature we shall meet again in other regions. Together with these and other anthropomorphic clay objects, the grave contained a large gold ornament repre- senting a highly stylized personage adorned with an intricate head-dress. The lower part consists of a crescent-shaped plaque, similar to a Peruvian *tumi* knife. Again, the calves of the legs are deformed by ligatures and two fantastic, crested animals are shown in profile, clinging to the arms of the figure. This object is now in the British Museum and a very similar one, also from Popayán and belonging to the Gold Museum in Bogotá, ap- pears in one of the plates.[43]

Plate 18

Following the Cauca on its northward course, we find a number or archaeological cultures which are still very little known but which, in essence, belong to the same level of slope- dwelling maize farmers who constituted small chiefdoms on the foot-hills and mountain folds of the neighbouring cordilleras.

In the region of Cali three ceramic complexes have been identified: Pichindé, Río Bolo, and Quebrada Seca, all of them
named after the small mountain streams on whose banks the
main excavations were carried out on house platforms and
graves.[44] Burials were found in shaft graves with side chambers,
with a circular, semicircular, or elliptical ground plan, most of
them on the crest-line of hills. At Pichindé the shafts of most
burials were found to be stacked with large stones. The pottery
from these burials shows distinctive features in all three instances.
The scanty grave goods from Pichindé include a coarse, sand-
tempered, globular type of pottery which was occasionally used
for burial urns. A number of conical spindle whorls were also
found. The Río Bolo wares are also sand-tempered and many
of the vessels have a red slip. Shapes include globular and sub-
globular cooking vessels, pedestal pots and bowls, and other
simple forms. The most elaborate complex is Quebrada Seca.
One of the shaft graves contained five extended burials accompanied by 260 pottery vessels, and several other graves, too, contained large amounts of pottery. Most of the containers are red-
slipped, occasionally with un-slipped bands near the rim. A
common form is a pedestal jar adorned with irregular incisions,
appliqué elements, or modelled human faces. Hemispherical
and pedestal bowls also occur. The three complexes from Cali
show no affiliations with Tierradentro, Calima, or 'Quimbaya'
wares. Probably they are comparatively recent, at most a few
centuries before the Spanish conquest.

North of Cali and east of the Calima area, at the foot of the
Western Cordillera, lie the villages of Yotoco and Vijes. In the
vicinity of these villages some finds made by treasure-hunters
have produced ceramics which do not seem to be related to the
Calima and 'Quimbaya' complexes, but which bear witness to
a high development of the potter's art. A quite characteristic
style consists of anthropomorphic vessels of globular shape. The
short, convex-walled neck represents the head and the features

Fig. 45. *Anthropomorphic vessel
from Yotoco; Valle district*

are made of appliqué strips or pellets. The face shows a mod‑
elled curved nose, 'coffee bean' eyes, and ears with plug‑shaped
ornaments. This brown, burnished ware is quite different from
the Calima ceramics found just east of Yotoco, but may be
related to some of the little‑known ceramic complexes of the
Central Cordillera and also to Quebrada Seca. Conical spindle
whorls of stone, adorned with engraved lines and dots, also
differ from the more usual clay whorls of this area.[45]

No systematic excavations have been carried out in the dis‑
trict of Antioquia although this must undoubtedly be a crucial
area in Colombia.[46] At the time of the Spanish conquest the
mountains and valleys of this region were densely populated by
Indians who had formed large tribal confederations under their
local chieftains. The fertile well‑watered soils and the rich gold‑
mines of Antioquia, together with its strategic location as a con‑
tact area, provided a most propitious background for higher
cultural development, but unfortunately the prehistory of this
part of the country is still unknown. Many private and museum
collections contain objects of pottery, gold, and stone which
suggest relationships with the Calima and 'Quimbaya' areas,
but the many pottery styles to be discerned also suggest much

Fig. 45

Fig. 46

135

regional variation and considerable time-depth. The six-teenth-century chronicler Juan Bautista Sardela, in his account of the conquest of Antioquia by Captain Jorge Robledo, mentions a tantalizing discovery. Somewhere in the desolate valley of Arbi, reconnoitring Spanish troops found '... very large ancient buildings, all in ruins, and roads of dressed stone, made by human hands, larger than those of Cuzco, and cabins in the manner of store houses.' Alas, we do not know the location of the 'valley of Arbi'. Large areas of Antioquia are still heavily forested and it may well be that somewhere under the thick jungle growth, there lie the ruins of a major architectural complex.[46]

Let us now cross the Central Cordillera and enter the wide Magdalena valley. Here and there, on the flood-plain and on the neighbouring slopes, there are house sites, graves, and other remains which prove that maize-farming communities of Formative type had colonized this region for many centuries. The upper and middle courses of the Magdalena are still too little known, but stray finds from many sites suggest the presence of fairly large riverine villages and a considerable advance in pottery and metallurgy. However, cultures of clearly defined Sub-Andean level have not been found yet in this part of the country, and mounds or other indications of major ceremonial complexes are so far unknown.

By the end of the first millennium AD, a major change seems to have taken place in religious practices over much of Colombia, at least as far as burial rites were concerned. We now find a pattern of urn-burials, sometimes accompanied by cremation but more often as the simple re-burial of disarticulated bones. Often these urns, dozens or even hundreds of them, form large cemeteries near village sites; at other times they are found in small groups of three or four only, on hill-tops, in caves, or within the area of house sites. At times such groups of urns are found in shaft graves with side chambers. There are many different kinds of urns. The most common form is a large ovoid

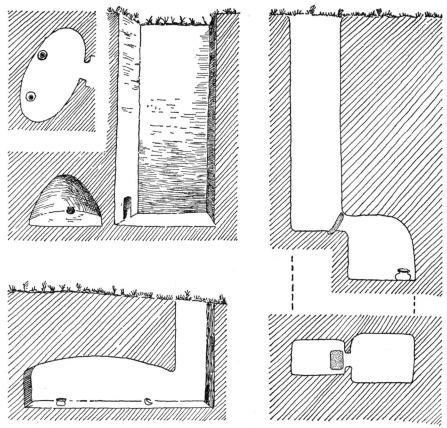

Fig.. 46. Types of shaft graves from the Western Cordillera

vessel with an orifice wide enough to admit the skull, but there   Plate 33
are also globular or sub-globular urns, large cylindrical containers, and elaborate urns with composite silhouettes adorned
with biomorphic handles and painted or incised decoration.
Often the face or the entire figure of the buried person is represented on the body of the urn or on the lid. On the upper and
middle Magdalena the common ovoid urns often have faces
made of appliqué strips while in the foot-hills of the Sierra   *Fig. 47*
Nevada the face or the entire head is represented on the hemi-

spherical lid. From the middle course of the Magdalena come
Plate 34 large urns covered with incised designs and with a modelled
figurine sitting on a bench on top of the lid. The large cemeteries
of Tamalameque, on the lower Magdalena, are formed of shaft
graves the side chambers of which contain groups of cylindrical
Plates 35, 36 urns with lids fashioned in the shape of large heads. Often these
anthropomorphic urns represent warriors armed with clubs and
adorned with many personal ornaments, recalling the figurines
from Popayán, with their shields and crested helmets, to which
they bear a distinct resemblance. Many of these anthropomorphic urns even show the same artificial deformation of the calves
as was first observed on the figurines from Popayán.

This urn-burial horizon extends over immense areas: from
the Guajira to Darien, from the upper Cauca river to the Orinoco, along the rivers, on the hill-tops and ridges, always near
shallow midden sites which contain the ceramic and lithic materials characteristic of small maize-farming settlements. Who,
then, were these peoples who buried their dead in those strange
vessels containing the remains of the warriors and chiefs we see
sitting stiffly on their little stools, hands on knees, their bodies
covered with strings of beads? It is possible that the custom of
secondary urn-burial developed in lowland Colombia, on the
level of Formative tribes, and that it spread as a religious complex which was accepted, eventually, by some of the Sub-Andean groups. But perhaps this new ritual was introduced by
another, less developed culture. The grave goods found with
the urn-burials are not very distinctive; they rarely include
elaborate objects of clay or gold, and if they do, the artifacts are
of poor workmanship. Rather, we find a few nose-rings of copper, necklace beads of shell, coarse clay spindle whorls, and
a few stone celts associated with this kind of burial; but no
elaborate vessels or hoards of metal objects.[47]

At the time of the Spanish conquest, many agricultural tribes
of Colombia were threatened by attack from another invader:

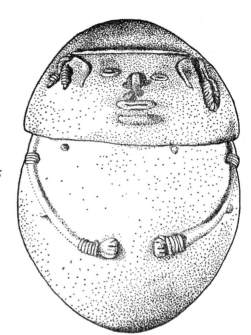

Fig. 47. *Effigy burial urn from La Mesa;*
Tairona area

the Caribs. Some of these fierce Indians, penetrating from the
Guianas and the Venezuelan coast, had already established
themselves in the Colombian lowlands and had conquered the
small villages and some of the mountain folds of the interior
provinces. It is possible that it was they who contributed to the
spread of the urn-burial pattern. This process may have extended over many centuries and though some of the urn-burials
seem to be quite old, the general characteristics are those of a
recent development. Some authors have correlated the urn-
burials with Carib invaders, pointing out that the deformation
of the calves, produced by ligatures, is a Carib custom.[48]

Urn-burial was practised until recent times by several Colombian tribes of different stages of cultural development. We
may quote here short descriptions of this practice as observed
by two sixteenth-century chroniclers. Oviedo, referring to

139

the Indians of Cartagena, says: '... and once the flesh is gone and the bones are clean, they paint them red, and then they put them, thus painted, into vessels or jars, and in this manner they keep them inside the house, or outside it.'[49] Pedro de Aguado gives a more colourful description from the Guayupe, a tribe of the eastern plains: 'If the dead man is a cacique or a principal chieftain or a person who necessarily has to have a successor, they put the corpse into a ... hollow tree trunk for a coffin and put fire to it till the flames consume it and convert the corpse to dust and ashes and this they put into a vessel or pot and, keeping the bones apart, they grind them and put them into another vessel... and taking the vessels with the ashes of the dead they arrange them and adorn them with the jewels and finery he had used and owned during life and take them to the house where the people have gathered and in the middle of the house they put them on a seat on which the dead person used to sit when alive... And when this is done, two or three of the dead man's closest relatives get up and lifting the seat with the vessels on their shoulders they begin to dance...'[50]

A few words must be said here about the many engraved and painted rocks found in Colombian territory.[51] We can distinguish two types: petroglyphs, i.e. designs produced by pecking or scratching on a rock surface; and pictographs, in which the designs were painted with mineral or vegetable colours. Both types are common in Colombia but there are certain differences in distribution; Chibcha territory is characterized by pictographs painted in red, while in the inter-Andean valleys engraved petroglyphs predominate. East of the cordilleras, in the Orinoco and Amazon basins, both types are found. Petroglyphs are mostly found on isolated boulders and outcrops, often on water-worn rock-surfaces, and generally cover a horizontal or only slightly inclined area. Pictographs are more often found on vertical walls in rock shelters, where the designs are somewhat protected. Both geometric and naturalistic designs occur; the

Plates 64, 65

first category includes parallel or undulating lines, rhomboid elements, concentric squares or circles, spirals, triangles, dotted areas, and so on. The naturalistic forms represent human beings and animals such as frogs, snakes, birds, or mammals. There are also 'sun faces' and representations of monstrous beings wearing elaborate head-dresses. It is possible that some of the pictographs and petroglyphs were connected with religious practices but most of them seem to be occasional 'doodles' made by people who happened to spend some time near a conspicuous boulder or under a rock-shelter. We know nothing about the chronological position of this art form and only in the case of the highland Chibcha, where the distribution of the pictographs coincides with the tribal territory, can we suggest a correlation with a specific group of peoples. Areas where there is a high concentration of petroglyphs are the Cauca valley, the district of Antioquia, and part of the western slopes of the Eastern Cordillera. No engraved or painted rocks have been reported from the Pacific coast, the Guajira Peninsula, and the lower Magdalena, and in the Caribbean lowlands they are extremely rare. East of the cordilleras there are many places on the tributaries of the Orinoco and upper Amazon, where both types of this art form are quite frequent.

CHAPTER VIII

The Village Federations

AMONG THE WIDE ARRAY of scattered village farmers and local valley chiefdoms, two cultural units stand out in protohistoric and historic times: The Tairona of the Sierra Nevada of Santa Marta and the Chibcha of the highlands surrounding Bogotá. Encircled on all sides by tribes of a much lower cultural level, indeed by hostile groups more like encroaching 'barbarians' than dependent neighbours, these two cultures achieved a somewhat wider political cohesion. One can hardly speak here of 'incipient states', much less of 'kingdoms' or 'empires'; rather, they were strong village federations in which a large number of settlements and peoples of the same ethnic stock were united under the control of a single individual, a powerful chieftain who often combined political and military leadership with the functions and status of a high priest. In both regions, the Andean highlands and the Sierra Nevada, a dense population, fertile soils, an efficient technology, and integrated religious systems, mark new steps, a new level of advance which began to outgrow even the Sub-Andean stage of the other chiefdoms. Although the Tairona and Chibcha have much in common, at least in so far as their general level of socio-religious and technological complexity is concerned, they also vary a great deal in details of culture content and emphasis. Owing to differences in their physical surroundings, in their technological equipment, in their local traditions, and in their contacts with other peoples, they developed divergent orientations and we must, therefore, discuss them separately.

For the Sierra Nevada we have a fairly full archaeological record.[52] The Tairona were a lowland tribe occupying the foothills of the mountains and rarely populating areas above an altitude of 1,000 m. The dense population lived in large nucleated villages situated in the mountain folds, often in a strategic position for easy defence. The principal towns were Bonda and Pocigueica, both inhabited by thousands of Indians, and for some of the valleys the chronicles mention hundreds and even thousands of houses. The Spaniards marvelled at the architecture of the Tairona; Juan de Castellanos writes: 'To reach [the villages] one has to climb stairs of well-dressed and placed stone slabs... the villages are near streams, with their streets well traced and ordered, and strong and well-built houses...'[53] A ceremonial structure is described thus: '... there was a well-built structure with six or seven landings, each one *vara* high, and a narrow stairway in the middle in order to ascend, from whence they watched the spectacles which took place below in a wide and well-paved court.'[54] Only the house foundations, retaining walls, and stairs were built of stone; the houses and temples themselves were circular structures of wood, but of a size and workmanship which impressed the Spaniards. Large slab-paved roads connected one village with another and long flights of stairs ascended the steep slopes.

The economic basis of Tairona society was maize farming, and this and many other food plants were grown in irrigated fields and terraces. The Spaniards found: '... cultivated gardens and the fields they irrigated with ditches dug in an admirable order, in the same way as the men of Lombardy and the Etruscans cultivate and irrigate theirs.'[55] There was an active trade between villages, those of the mountain valleys trading gold and cotton cloth for fish and salt from the coastal settlements. Certain articles such as necklace beads, for the manufacture of which the Tairona were famous, were traded as far as Chibcha territory, and from there emeralds were brought down to the coast.

In the early sixteenth century a large number of villages had become united under the leadership of certain chieftains and two rival confederations. These, Bonda, in the foot-hills near the modern Santa Marta, and Pocigueica, in a mountain stronghold, had begun to dominate the surrounding country, side. Internal struggles for power also seem to have developed between the civil and military authority of the caciques, and an influential class of priests *(naoma),* a circumstance the Spaniards took good advantage of. The Tairona were an extremely war, like people but military leadership was disorganized and, as a rule, every village led its own guerrilla warfare, rarely joining forces with others. Distinguished warriors *(manicatos)* wore special insignia and it is said that Pocigueica was defended by an army of twenty thousand. Religious practices were not de, scribed in much detail by the chroniclers. All villages had temples and ceremonial houses where the people 'worshipped the devil' and there were large ceremonial centres in the moun, tains whither pilgrimages were made in a manner which caused the Spaniards to refer to one of them mockingly as 'New Rome'. Several types of burial customs are described: smoke, drying of the corpse, secondary urn, burial, and burial in 'vaults', but it is possible that these data refer to different stages of a single ritual.

It took the Spaniards the better part of a century to subdue the Tairona who, after periods of uneasy peace, rebelled again and again against the foreign invader. The last great rebellion occurred in 1599 and was suppressed in 1600, after three months of fierce battles in which all resistance was broken and the tribe ceased to exist as a unit. Spanish troops burned and sacked the villages, devastating the fields and taking prisoner all chieftains and their relatives, except those who had been able to escape into the mountain fastnesses.

We must now turn to the archaeological evidence for this culture which, in many ways, achieved the highest stage of de, velopment among the Sub, Andean aborigines of Colombia. Surface sites with architectural or technological features are plentiful over much of the northern and western flanks of the

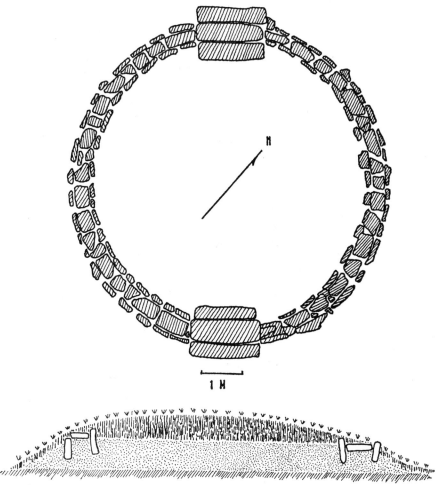

Fig. 48.   Ground-plan and cross-section of Tairona house; Pueblito site

Sierra Nevada. The village units, varying in size from a few
houses to several hundreds, are rarely found on flat ground but
are located rather on slopes and ridges with interconnected clus-
ters of houses often covering large areas. Typical of these villages

Fig. 48

are the 'ring' house platforms consisting of dressed or rough stones set in a circle, the diameter of which may be as much as 20 m. Often the house occupies a low mound surrounded by a retaining wall of rough stones, through which a short staircase leads up to the flat surface. The house foundations consist of one or more concentric circles of stones, sometimes of short vertical slabs, or simply of boulders set close together. In the best-built foundations a number of wedge-shaped, horizontally superimposed slabs were cut to fit the arc of the circle and form a wide ring. All houses have two doors, on opposite sides, marked by large slabs which are often particularly well dressed; smaller slabs arranged in steps lead from there toward the outside. Sometimes several houses occupy a single terrace or low mound, with two or more stairs traversing the retaining walls. There are also mounds of triangular or circular shape; these are faced on all sides with slabs and do not seem to have been house foundations. In most larger village sites the individual houses are grouped around one or more ceremonial structures. These consist of particularly large and well-made circular foundations, sometimes provided with four doors, the entire structure being located on a large terrace or on a flat stretch of ground in a valley bottom. They are often provided with causeways, stairs, pillars, and stone tables or benches set on smaller blocks. Several large temple structures on the Córdoba river have a square ground plan, the nucleus being a small hill whose sides have been covered with vertical walls. At times the front is stepped and several staircases lead up to the platform on top of the structure. Small streams and rivulets crossing the terrain of a village site flow between stretches of walls built of rough stones. A single slab, from bank to bank, might serve as a bridge or this may consist of a more complex structure, the slab serving only as a base for a fill of boulders on top of which lie several flat stones. Square stone-lined water reservoirs are found not only in village sites but also in the vicinity of uninhabited

Plate 49

Plate 48

Fig. 49

Fig. 50

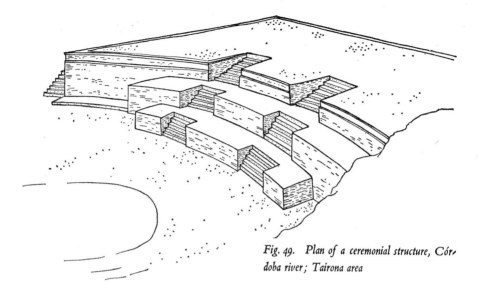

Fig. 49. *Plan of a ceremonial structure, Cór,*
doba river; Tairona area

beaches, and slab-lined drainage ditches, sometimes with a
covering, are found in some village areas.

Excavation of these house sites and the surrounding patio
areas has brought to light a rich record of how the early
inhabitants lived. Pottery and stone artifacts abound, and
their nature and distribution allow us a glimpse of everyday life. It seems that each house was occupied by a single nu-
clear family. The fireplace, consisting of three or four stones,

Fig. 50. *Detail of bridge construction; Tairona area*

was located slightly nearer the back door than the front, where the main entrance looked out over the valley or towards the next stream. By careful excavation of the trampled earth-floor it has been possible to recover the cooking vessels near the hearth, the small hammer-stones and grinding pestles used in preparing food, and the large water containers standing near-by against the wall. The centre of the house is clean and free of furniture, but along the curve of the wall there lie the odds and ends which once belonged to each member of the family and which were left lying on the floor or dropped down from bags or baskets hanging on the rafters or posts. In a corner there will be a few polished stone celts, a fish-hook of stone, net-sinkers, a couple of bird-shaped clay whistles and perhaps some ceremonial object such as a finely polished monolithic axe. That the opposite side of the house was occupied by the women is suggested by the pottery, the children's necklaces, and the scraping and grinding tools of daily food preparation.

The ethnography of the Indian tribes still surviving in the Sierra Nevada of Santa Marta has provided valuable clues for the interpretation of some archaeological finds.[56] For example, in many house sites, when we were digging below the floor or under the stone slabs of the door, we found carefully buried pottery vessels. Sometimes these vessels were enclosed in a small box-like cist made of thin slabs, or they were buried in a hole and the mouth of the pot was carefully covered with a stone disk. The discovery of such a well-hidden pot makes one, of course, suspect some valuable cache but, disappointingly, these vessels proved to contain only a handful of pebbles, or of various necklace beads of stone. The significance of these caches was unknown until we observed the survival of this custom among the Cogui Indians, who are the modern descendants of the Tairona. Among the Cogui, every time a house is being built, a pottery vessel is buried ceremonially in the foundations. For each member of the household a small pebble is deposited in the vessel, varying in size, colour, and shape according to the specific magical attributes of each matrilineal or patrilineal kin. At the birth of a child, the pot is dug up and a new pebble is added; in this manner all the inhabitants are identified and taken under the protection of the spirits which are the guardians of the dwelling. While excavating a ceremonial structure, we discovered near the main entrance the skull of a jaguar, a find we were unable to interpret at that time. Among the Cogui, however, we learned that all ceremonial houses are dedicated to the jaguar-god *Cashindúcua*, and that in ancient times jaguar skulls adorned the doors of these houses. The following is another parallel: quite often one finds in Tairona sites some miniature grinding stones and mullers, together with broken necklace beads and bits of coloured stone. Among the modern Cogui these objects are still in use. Certain pebbles or beads are ground and pulverized, and the powder represents 'food' for ancestral spirits or divinities. Other objects frequently found in Tairona territory are thin, wing-shaped bars of well-polished stone which, we thought, were pendants to be worn around the neck. Some Cogui priests still own such objects and they are in fact musical instruments. Suspended in pairs from the elbows of a person dancing with slightly uplifted arms, these thin plates produce a tinkling sound and are still used in certain ceremonies. These few examples, then, not only show the remarkable continuity of Tairona culture, but are ample proof of the many clues ethnographic parallels can provide in the interpretation of otherwise problematic archaeological finds.

Tairona pottery is complex and elaborate. Culinary vessels and the many containers used in food preparation and storage consist of a rather coarse red ware which, although it is well finished and of pleasing shapes, is not outstanding in any special way. A number of other types of ware, however, show an extraordinary development of the potter's art. A burnished black ware is most characteristic. Shapes include tetrapod bowls with

Fig. 51

bulbous hollow supports, pedestal or ring-base cups, and a great variety of shouldered composite-silhouette vessels. Some vessel shapes seem to have been used exclusively as containers for offerings in burials or caches. They take the form of cylindrical jars of red or black ware, with fitted covers which rest upon a projecting sub-labial flange. Decoration consists mainly of modelling, appliqué strips, incision and excision; painted decoration is extremely rare. Many red-ware vessels are adorned on the neck with human faces formed from appliqué strips.

Fig. 52
Plate 52
Fig. 53

Zoomorphic vessels show jaguars, foxes, bats, snakes, turtles, and crocodiles. Among the most elaborate are very small containers: tetrapods with snake motifs, anthropomorphic vessels with fangs and protruding tongues, often recalling Mesoamer-

Fig. 54

ican Tlaloc representations; and small vessels with deep vertical grooves. Flat ladles, with a handle shaped like a penis, are frequent in the region of Bonda.

Fig. 55

Elaborate clay ocarinas constitute a special category of objects, ranging from simple bird shapes to very complex figurines

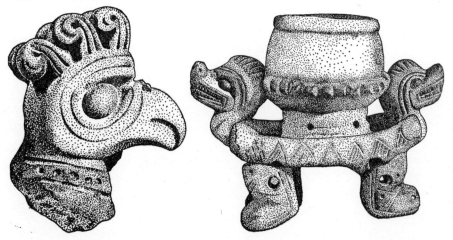

Fig. 51. Pottery fragment; Tairona area   *Fig. 52.   Zoomorphic vessel from the Tairona area*

Fig. 53. Miniature vessel; Tairona area *Fig. 54. Miniature vessel; Tairona area*

of warriors or priests, with high feathered head-dresses, nose ornaments, clubs, and other paraphernalia. Some of these effigies show people wearing animal masks or sometimes a human face peers through the open jaws of a jaguar or reptilian monster. Other clay objects are flat stamps with finely incised geometric or biomorphic motifs. Spindle whorls are lacking altogether and must have been made of some perishable material.

Plate 51

Fig. 56

Fig. 57

Fig. 55. Clay ocarina; Tairona area

151

Fig. 56. Masked figurine of clay (fragment); Tairona area
Fig. 57. Flat clay stamp; Tairona area

Large grinding stones, deeply hollowed and polished by long use, are found in profusion in house sites. Stone celts of trapez-oidal shape, and chisels of many different sizes are all extremely well made and even such common artifacts as net-sinkers and grinding implements are manufactured with care. The Tairona were skilful in the making of small stone carvings. Thousands of stone beads are found in house sites or in ceremonial caches, consisting of finely polished carnelian, agate, quartz, or other stones of pleasing colours. There are large tubular or spherical beads, buttons, Y- or bullet-shaped pendants, small disks, and a variety of biomorphic objects. On the upper Sevilla river, the central area of a ceremonial site contained a deposit more than a metre thick, of beads in all stages of manufacture. The upper-most layer was sealed off by a thick floor of burned clay. Mono-lithic axes, with both head and handle carved out of a single piece of stone, are quite common in caches and burials, as are also the wing-shaped objects mentioned above. Batons of pol-ished stone, from 20 to 45 cm. long, sometimes adorned with carved animal heads form part of this complex of ceremonial

Fig. 58

Fig. 59

Fig. 60

Fig. 58. Types of stone necklace beads and pendants; Tairona area

Fig. 59. Two monolithic axes of andesite; Tairona area

153

objects. A large stone mask with a protruding tongue was found in a covered jar near the stepped temple of the Córdoba river. Objects of jade-like translucent nephrite include stylized human figurines, bats with spread wings, or simple bar-shaped pendants.

Large stone carvings in the round are scarce but several roughly cylindrical or angular columns, with crude human faces carved or outlined on the surface, are known. Isolated stone heads are more frequent and are sometimes quite realistic; others are more stylized, like the one from Minca, near Santa Marta, which shows a carved face with a large mouth and a protruding tongue. Tairona metallurgy was highly developed and could vie with the best of Calima or Quimbaya craftsmanship. Hollow or open-cast figurines, nose ornaments, rings, beads, pendants, or bells are often made of an alloy rich in copper but are

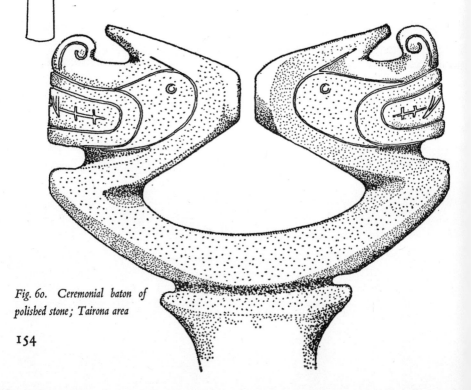

Fig. 60. Ceremonial baton of polished stone; Tairona area

Fig. 61. Large carved stone head from Minca; Tairona area
Fig. 62. Carved stone mask from the Córdoba river; Tairona area

covered with a thin layer of gold. Some of the finest figurines show fantastic beings, half jaguar, half man, adorned with large head-dresses and accompanied by snake or dragon-like motifs.

Life in a Tairona village must have been colourful and busy. Here were a people who loved to manufacture with care and taste the simplest utensils of everyday life, to decorate them and to individualize them. They took pleasure in the smooth and shining surfaces of their black pottery, of their stone artifacts, and of their gold and copper trinkets. There must assuredly have been skilled artisans in many different crafts: potters, gold-smiths, stone carvers, masons, and we can imagine the artistry of their wood carvings, textiles, and featherwork which gained the admiration of the Spaniards.

The end was foreshadowed when the first red sails of the Spanish galleons appeared on the horizon. To the bearded men who came ashore, sailors, soldiers, priests, miners, and account-

Plates 53, 54

Fig. 63

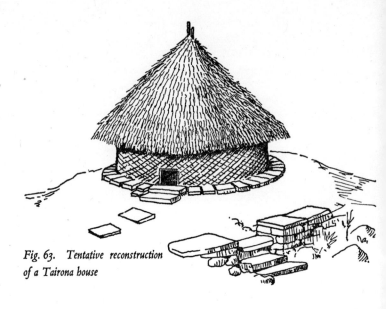

Fig. 63. Tentative reconstruction
of a Tairona house

ants, these Indians were idolatrous pagans, victims of the devil's
snares, sunk in ignorance and brutishness, who must be saved
from themselves and from their sinister gods. And then came
slavery and epidemics, tributes and forced labour, and the few
voices which could be heard in defence of this lost cause were
drowned in the clamour and excitement of discovery and conquest, or in the tedium of colonial administration and the de-
positions of scribes. Early in 1600, when the last battle had been
fought, the governor Juan Guiral Velón condemned the cap-
tive chieftains to death or exile. The chief *Cuchacique*, ring-
leader of the last rebellion, was ordered '... to be dragged by the
tails of two wild colts and torn into quarters and these put on
the trails, and the head put in a cage...' The governor's decree
goes on and on, citing the long list of Tairona chieftains: 'All
these Indians... I condemn and order to be hanged by their
necks... that he be strangled in the usual form and that his body
be burned in live flames till it be turned to ashes, so that no
memory be left of him...'[57]

We have described Tairona culture only in its protohistoric form because too little is known about its earlier phases. At Nahuanje, one of the inlets east of Santa Marta, several burial mounds were found to contain pottery which, on account of its shape and painted decoration, seems to represent an earlier time-level, perhaps related to our First Painted Horizon. Stray finds from the vicinity of Santa Marta consist of pottery which is related to this horizon and also to late Momil developments. However, the area whose pottery types appear to be closely re-lated to Tairona ware is the lower Magdalena, especially the Zambrano region. Quite possibly Tairona culture developed first in a riverine environment and moved toward the mountain valleys of the Sierra Nevada only in relatively recent times, per-haps under the threat of other warlike lowland tribes. But quite apart from this postulated riverine origin, Tairona culture seems to have received strong Meso- and Central American influ-ences, most probably by oversea contacts. Among the Cogui Indians, an isolated and little-acculturated Chibcha-speaking tribe of the Sierra Nevada, which seems to have carried on the essential Tairona tradition, we find the greatest Mesoamerican element content registered so far. The most arresting parallels are: emphasis on 'dawn' in creation myths; multiple creation of the universe and mankind; the concept of several stratified worlds difficult of access; association of colours, death and life forces, and theriomorphic beings with the four world quarters; special abode for those dying in childbirth or by drowning; reptilian origin of deities; duality (malevolent-benevolent) of deities; mono-polymorphism and quadruplicity of deities; jag-uar sun deity; masked dancers impersonating the deity; nine as a ritual number; illness attributed to sin; symbolism of 'broom' and 'sweeping' for forgiveness of sin; confession; divination by muscle twitching and fingernail tapping; a long training period for priests; a highly organized priesthood; the dog as a guide to the Beyond; careful observation of solstices and equinoxes, and astronomical markings. If, in the light of these data, we cast our minds back to the prehistoric Tairona and remember the stepped temples, the cylindrical jars with fitted lids, the elaborate figurines and many other associated elements, it seems reasonable to assume that it was not a question of the diffusion of isolated traits, but rather that these religious concepts and paraphernalia were transmitted as a complex. It would appear, therefore, that there existed a philosophic interrelation of religions, and that in the case of the Cogui we find the survival of an essentially Mesoamerican pattern in a still functioning culture of the Colombia mountain regions.

The Tairona culture is notable for showing – though in a very limited territory – the remains of an urban development, with large public works such as temples, agricultural terraces, irrigation, and paved roads. Nowhere else in Colombia do we find a similar advance in economic efficiency, architectural development, and religious integration. Only the narrow territorial expansion and the lack of political cohesion of the Tairona make their achievement inferior to that of the Chibcha of the highlands of the interior.

On the bleak elevated plateaux of Cundinamarca and Boyacá, the mountainous districts of the central part of the Eastern Cordillera, a large aboriginal population was flourishing by the early sixteenth century. The Chibcha, or Muisca as they called themselves, occupied the wide, fertile highland basins of Bogotá and Tunja, then, as now, regions of high population density. When in 1537 the first Spanish troops arrived in the highlands of Bogotá, after a gruelling march through regions which even today are still forbidding jungle, they found the Chibcha organized into two loose federations. While a chieftain with the title of *Zipa* controlled the southern part of the highlands, centred around Bogotá, another chieftain, called the *Zaque,* had his domain in the north, in the region of Tunja. The Spanish chroniclers wrote glowing reports of the Chibcha: of their 'kings' and nobles, their well-built palisaded villages, their wealth of gold and emeralds. They described Chibcha culture in a manner which gave the impression that they had found a truly civilized nation, almost on a par with the Mesoamerican or Central Andean states.

If one were to judge Chibcha culture only by the number and quality of the material remains that have been preserved in archaeological sites, it would be difficult indeed to assign to it the advanced status it has been given in most ancient and modern literature. Taken trait by trait: architecture, burials, pottery, metallurgy, and so on, it is obvious that several lowland chiefdoms of the Cauca valley, the Central Cordillera, or the Caribbean coast had achieved a similar or even a higher development. The historical sources show clearly that, in terms of political cohesion, social structure, religious complexity, and economic efficiency, Chibcha culture had evolved beyond the level of the neighbouring groups. Archaeological research, admittedly scanty but still sufficiently advanced to formulate the broad outlines of the situation, does not always confirm the image of a highly developed culture; but we must bear in mind that many of these advances were achieved on a level where no major material remains could have been preserved for the archaeological record.

We must summarize the principal aspects of Chibcha culture as we know it from early Spanish sources, before discussing its prehistoric basis. The Chibcha were an intensely agricultural people who had domesticated a number of highland crops; they grew at least two local types of potato and also *quinoa*, *ulluco*, *oca*, *topinambur*, and *cubios*, a tuberous nasturtium. Agricultural terraces were used occasionally. Trade relations were important and the Chibcha exchanged salt, emeralds, and cotton cloth for gold and other luxury articles, and periodic market-days were held at several villages. Although the *Zipa* and the *Zaque* were nominally the overlords of their respective

domains, local rivalries between village chiefs often led to alli-
ances and internal raids by which one local chieftain tried to
subdue the other's tributary Indians. The ruling class, whose
succession was matrilineal, lived in large and well-built houses
– 'palaces' as the chroniclers call them – and were carried about
in gold-covered litters. Both rulers and priests, the latter called
jeque, had to undergo a special training period before assuming
office, consisting of several years of reclusion in a temple where
they fasted, abstained from sexual contacts, and learned the religious history and esoteric practices of the tribal culture. Religion
centred on a sun cult; large temples and shrines were dedicated
to the sun and the moon, but lakes, caves, and hill-tops were
also considered sacred places. Idols of wood, stone, cotton or
gold were kept at these spots and offerings were made to them
in the form of golden figurines *(tunjos)* and emeralds. Incense
was burned and the priests used hallucinogenous plants. Human sacrifices were made to the sun, the victims being often
enslaved prisoners of war from neighbouring lowland tribes.
Special troops *(guechas)* were stationed at the borders of the tribal
territory and warfare against the neighbouring Panche tribe of
the Magdalena valley, not only with the purpose of obtaining
sacrificial victims but also to defend the agricultural land on the
temperate slopes, had become chronic. A special sacrifice made
use of children who were bought by Chibcha emissaries from a
certain region of the Orinoco plains and were trained as ritually
pure temple servants before they were sacrificed. The victim's
heart and viscera were cut out, as nourishment for the sun, and
the blood was sprinkled over the sanctuaries. In a sacrifice of
captives, similar in detail to the Mexican *tlacacaliztli,* the victim
was tied on top of a high pole and arrows were shot at him from
below. Sacrifices of children to promote rainfall, and bird sacrifices were also practised. The principal culture hero *Bochica*
is described as an old bearded man who lived a holy life and
taught the people many arts and crafts before ascending to the

sky. It is obvious from this brief outline that Chibcha culture contained many strong Mesoamerican elements, a fact we are again inclined to attribute to influences which penetrated from the Pacific coast.[58]

We shall turn now to the archaeological evidence which has been discovered, so far, in Chibcha territory.[59] Although the historic Chibcha are said to have lived in large towns and compact villages, not many signs of major population concentrations have been observed. It is possible that many sites have been destroyed over the years by intensive post-conquest agriculture, road-building, and irrigation channels, but still it is difficult to explain why there should be so very few village sites left. On some of the hills and mountain slopes surrounding Bogotá and Tunja there are scattered house sites, circular or semicircular in shape, marked by a few stones set in a circle and by stray sherds and grinding stones, but these remains hardly measure up to the large palisaded settlements the Spaniards claim to have found. Stone constructions, domestic or ceremonial, are very scarce. Near Tunja and at other places in the northern area, several fairly large enclosures have been known since the last century, consisting of roughly hewn columns set in a circle or following an elliptical ground plan. A number of post-holes indicate that these columns had originally been combined with a wooden structure, and a large hole in the centre of one of these enclosures marks the point where a central post stood. Excavation of these enclosures did not bring to light much additional information. There were a few potsherds and grinding stones, and at the foot of one column an infant had been buried, perhaps a human sacrifice in the construction of a temple or a chief's house, a ritual described by the chroniclers. Isolated columns, some of them with notches and recesses at one end have been reported from the vicinity of Tunja, but nothing is known of the burial or pottery associations.[60] The famous 'Temple of the Sun' at Sogamoso (the ancient Sugamuxi) was a similar round structure made entirely of wood. It was burned by the Spaniards. The building has been reconstructed by archaeologists, together with several small huts and flexed burials in pit-graves, which were found in the immediate vicinity, but even this site, so often quoted in the early sources, seems to have been hardly more than a tribal ceremonial house or the dwelling of a local chief.[61] Chibcha house and midden sites lack time-depth; the deposits, which are very shallow and cover a small area, are not to be compared with Sub-Andean, or even many Formative sites of the lowlands. This could be explained perhaps in terms of a frequent shifting of villages, but there is no evidence for this type of settlement pattern either, all village sites being scarce. We must conclude, then, that the Chibcha arrived on the highlands at a comparatively late date and that they never lived in large permanent villages but formed a scattered rural population. The main features of their culture are unlikely to have originated within their historic habitat, but where these developments took place we do not know. Perhaps in the Magdalena valley, or in the mountain ranges of the north, toward Venezuela; these are guesses, nothing more. So far, no cultural remains suggesting they might be ancestral to protohistoric Chibcha culture are known from the lowlands, but this means little if we remember the dearth of systematic excavations in the middle and upper Magdalena regions.

It is possible that certain objects from the highlands may belong to an earlier time-level, namely the figurines of stone which have been discovered in the mud banks of the lagoon of Fuquene, north of Bogotá. In 1941 the lake level began to drop and in the cracked mud there appeared small loaf-shaped blocks of soft stone, roughly shaped in the form of human effigies with incised features. They may be votive offerings to a lake-dwelling spirit, a religious concept quite familiar to the historic Chibcha. Plates 55, 56 Still farther to the north, in the caves of La Belleza, were found large quantities of small anthropomorphic figurines probably

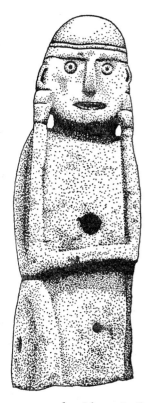

Fig. 64. *Large stone statues from Mongua; Chibcha area*

connected with a similar ritual. They are made of soft stone and show highly stylized human shapes in sitting or crouching positions, some of them resting on little four-legged stools. We have no means of dating these two figurine complexes of, probably, votive offerings and to call them 'earlier' because they look more 'primitive' may be quite erroneous.

In 1964 a major discovery was made near Mongua, in the Sogamoso district. In this isolated mountain village situated almost 3,000 m. above sea level, agricultural labourers found in a field six large anthropomorphic statues of stone, roughly cylindrical in shape, their extremities and heads carved in relief. Similar statues have been reported from Socha Vieja, another mountain village of this area.[62]

Fig. 64

Chibcha burials fall into several categories; among them, cave burials in which one or several corpses were deposited in deep caves or rock shelters, often accompanied by a few grave goods, form a distinct category. The bodies were tied in cloth or rough netting, in a crouching or sitting position, with knees drawn up to the chin and arms folded over the chest. Quite often these corpses are well preserved, having been eviscerated and smoke-dried. Grave goods consist of pottery, spindle whorls of stone, loom swords, wooden spear-throwers provided with stone hooks, and odd pieces of wood and textiles. Sometimes the corpse is found sitting on a wooden bench. Some of these cave burials, for example those of Los Santos go back to the twelfth century. The mummy of a child, discovered near Sibaté, was found to be adorned with a crown of parrot feathers and from its neck hung a small calabash and a *millefiori* bead, proving that this type of burial survived till historic times. Slab-covered graves or pit-graves without covering are found occasionally and in the latter type the body is often buried in a flexed position. Shaft graves with side chambers seem to be unknown in Chibcha territory, but secondary urn-burial in plain globular vessels has been reported.

Plate 57

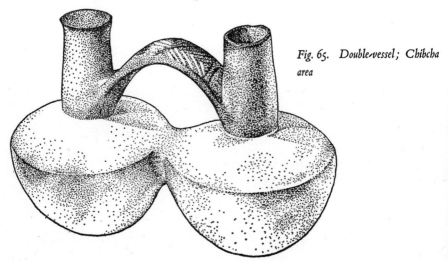

Fig. 65.   *Double-vessel; Chibcha area*

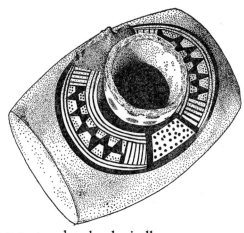

Fig. 66. Barrel-shaped vessel; Chibcha area

Chibcha pottery, although competent and technologically well made, is far less elaborate than most of the pottery from the lowland chiefdoms. Monochrome ware, dark brown, red, gray, or orange, is the rule, and coarse sand or ground sherds are the usual tempering materials. The commonest shapes are cooking pots, often with two or even four handles which connect the rim with the upper part of the container. Pedestal bowls, some-times with slightly flaring rims, are also common, and so are globular vessels with tall cylindrical necks. Double-vessels and so-called shoe-shaped vessels too are frequently encountered. Much of Chibcha ceramic is undecorated. When decorated wares do occur they are often painted in red on an orange, white, or cream background and sometimes we find two-colour painting in red and white on an orange base. The designs, paint-ed or incised, generally take the form of parallel lines, triangles, spiral-shaped elements, concentric circles, and dotted areas. An-thropomorphic or zoomorphic representations in painting are rare but occasionally the tall neck of a jar is adorned with a human face or the interior of a bowl is decorated with stylized animal figures. Anthropomorphic figurines or vessels are very distinctive in style. Shield-shaped human faces are characteris-tic, the eyes and lips consisting of horizontal bars and the mod-elled nose wearing a large square ornamental plaque. Some of

Plates 58, 60, 61

Fig. 65

Fig. 66

Plates 59, 62

these figurines show warriors holding spear-throwers or clubs, and wearing ornate head-dresses or strings of beads carried bandolier fashion. A few hollow figurines were found to contain objects of gold. As a whole, Chibcha art conveys an impression of stiffness and symmetry, quite unlike the 'baroque' shapes of many lowland styles.

Fig. 67

Small objects of stone are often well finished and have pleasing shapes, decorated with profuse incisions. Stone spindle whorls of many different forms, often disk-shaped, bear incised designs filled with a white pigment, and small necklace beads

Fig. 68

or amulets occur in the shape of birds, fish, reptiles, or stylized human figures. Relief carvings of small frogs, birds, or humans served as moulds for gold-work and are often well proportioned

Fig. 69

and highly polished. Chibcha gold objects show the stiff, two-dimensional quality of much of the decoration found in clay and stone. Characteristic are human figurines of elongated trian-

Fig. 70
Plate 63

gular shape, consisting of a thin plate with wire-like features in relief, made by the *cire-perdue* technique. The same technique is used for animal figures, crowns, sceptres, and a multitude of small objects often found as votive offerings in caves or lakes. Chibcha metallurgy was far less advanced technologically and aesthetically than that of most lowland tribes.

Fig. 67.   Stone spindle whorls with incised designs ; Chibcha area

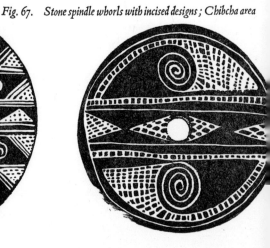

Fig. 68. Relief-carved stone mould for gold-work; Chibcha area

It will be seen, then, that the archaeological finds do not give the impression of a highly advanced culture. But by the very nature of our evidence we can, of course, reconstruct only a very partial picture of the past. Many of the advanced features of Chibcha culture left no material remains and for them we must take the word of the chroniclers. It seems that the Spaniards were impressed by the large population, by the climate and landscape, in many ways so similar to that of Castile; and by the peaceful peasant life of the Indians who soon submitted to the rule of the conquerors. On the other hand, it is evident that by establishing the Spanish capital at Bogotá, there was more contact with and more interest in aboriginal culture there than in other early foundations. This led, perhaps, to a certain bias, as compared with the attitudes shown towards other tribes. The Chibcha soon became docile tributary Indians and their country proved highly productive for the new crops and cattle the Spaniards introduced. The legend of El Dorado, combined with the wealth in natural resources and manpower of the rising kingdom of New Granada, contributed to the myth of Chibcha 'civilization', a myth which has persisted down the centuries, but which still lacks the evidence of archaeological fact.

But what of El Dorado? High up in the mountains behind Bogotá, there lies a small lake, the sacred lake of Guatavita.

*Fig. 69.
Spear-thrower
books of stone;
Chibcha area*

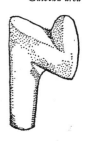

167

Fig. 70.
Flat gold
figurine;
Chibcha area

This spot in the desolate Andean highlands was a place of worship for the Chibcha, a place where a supreme power dwelt. Each time a new chieftain was to take office he had to be consecrated at this lake in a splendid ceremony. While on the shores thousands of Indians gathered and huge fires burned on the surrounding heights, the new cacique entered a raft loaded with offerings and was rowed to the middle of the lake. His naked body had been coated with a resin and then covered from head to foot with gold dust, till he was transformed into a gleaming statue. Then, while the crowd tossed offerings into the water and the bonfires blazed toward the sky, the cacique submerged himself and when he rose again his golden load had been washed off his body and had descended like rain to the bottom of the lake. Returning to the shore he was acclaimed by his people as the new overlord.

It was here that the legend of El Dorado was born, the imagery of the Gilded Man whose treasures became the symbol of the wealth of the Indies and the fateful star which led armies and fleets in pursuit of a phantom. We all know of the glories and the sufferings of this search. But what was the origin of this strange ritual? What was the meaning of the gilded body diving into the depths of a mountain lake? To answer this question we must leave behind the enchanted world of Indian legend and turn to the prosaic facts of geology.[63]

It seems that several thousand years ago, certainly at a time when man already roamed the cordilleras, a huge meteorite fell at Guatavita and buried itself in this lonely mountain landscape. A fiery mass, a blinding flash of gold dropped out of the sky and shook the earth while roaring thunder echoed over the Andes. A golden god had descended and had choosen his abode in the depths of this land. This, then, is the powerful spirit which dwells at the bottom of Lake Guatavita and this is what the gilded cacique symbolizes when he dives into the waters to acquire the power to lead his people.

Notes on the Text

Abbreviations

AA   *American Antiquity,* Washington

BA   *Boletín de Arqueología,* Bogotá

BG   *Boletín de Geología,* Bucaramanga

BIA   *Boletín del Instituto de Antropología,* Medellín

DE   *Divulgaciones Etnológicas,* Barranquilla

ES   *Etnologiska Studier,* Göteborg

GM   *Geologie en Mijnbouw,* The Hague

RACC   *Revista de la Academia Colombiana de Ciencias Exactas, Físicas y Naturales,* Bogotá

RCA   *Revista Colombiana de Antropología,* Bogotá

RI   *Revista de las Indias,* Bogotá

RIEN   *Revista del Instituto Etnológico Nacional,* Bogotá

ZE   *Zeitschrift für Ethnologie,* Brunswick

CHAPTER I

1 For a recent appraisal of the Intermediate Area see the various papers of the symposium 'Los problemas de los territorios entre las culturas meso-americanas y andinas' published in Actas del XXXIII Congreso Internacional de Americanistas, San José, 1958, I, 105–210 (San José, 1959). See also Clarence L. Hay (editor), *The Maya and Their Neighbors,* (New York, 1940), especially the papers by Samuel K. Lothrop, Philip Ainsworth Means and Alfred Kidder II.

2 The principal Spanish chroniclers and their works are: Juan de Castellanos, *Elegías de varones ilustres,* (Madrid, 1847) and *Historia del Nuevo Reino de Granada,* (Madrid, 1886); Fray Pedro Aguado, *Recopilación Historial,* 4 vol., (Bogotá, 1956–57); Gonzalo Fernández de Oviedo y Valdés, *Historia general y natural de las Indias, islas y tierrafirme del mar océano,* 4 vol., (Madrid, 1851–55); Pedro Cieza de León, *La crónica del Perú,*

(Madrid, 1862); Fray Pedro Simón, *Noticias historiales de las conquistas de Tierra Firme en las Indias Occidentales,* 5 vol., (Bogotá, 1882–92); Lucas Fernández de Piedrahita, *Historia general de las conquistas del Nuevo Reino de Granada,* (Bogotá, 1881); Antonio Herrera y Tordesillas, *Historia general de los hechos de los castellanos en las islas i tierra firme del mar océano,* 9 vol., (Madrid, 1726–27). Important collections of documents are, among others: Antonio B. Cuervo (editor), *Colección de documentos inéditos sobre la geografía y la historia de Colombia,* 4 vol., (Bogotá, 1891–94) and Juan Friede (editor), *Documentos inéditos para la historia de Colombia,* 9 vol., (Bogotá, 1955–60).

3 For a short outline of the history of archaeological research in Colombia see Luis Duque Gómez, *Colombia: Monumentos históricos y arqueológicos,* 2 vol., Instituto Panamericano de Geografía e Historia, (Mexico, 1955).

4 The principal authors who have postulated a division into 'archaeological areas' are, in chronological order: Thomas A. Joyce, *South American Archaeology,* (London, 1912); J. Eric Thompson, *Archaeology of South America,* Field Museum of Natural History, Anthropological Leaflet, No. 33, (Chicago, 1936); Gregorio Hernández de Alba, *Colombia: Compendio arqueológico,* (Bogotá, 1938); J. W. Schottelius, 'Estado actual de la arqueología colombiana', in *Educación*, I, 9–24, (Bogotá, 1941); Wendell C. Bennett, *Archaeological Regions of Colombia: A Ceramic Survey,* Yale University Publications in Anthropology, No. 30, (New Haven, 1944); *id.,* 'The Archaeology of Colombia', in *Handbook of South American Indians,* 2, 823–850, Bureau of American Ethnology, Bulletin 143, (Washington, 1946); Horst Nachtigall, *Indianerkunst der Nord-Anden,* (Berlin, 1961); *id., Alt-Kolumbien: Vorgeschichtliche Indianerkulturen,* (Berlin, 1961).

Chapter II

5 No modern geography of Colombia exists. The best work is still Pablo Vila, *Nueva geografía de Colombia,* (Bogotá, 1945). Regional geographies of importance are: Raymond E. Crist, *The Cauca Valley,* (Baltimore,

1952); Robert C. West, *The Pacific Lowlands of Colombia: A Negroid Area of the American Tropics,* (Baton Rouge, 1957); Ernesto Guhl, 'Ambiente geográfico⁄humano de la costa del Atlántico', *Revista Geográfica,* I, 139–172, (Barranquilla, 1952). Other pertinent publications are: Herbert Wilhelmy, 'Die klimamorphologische und pflanzengeographische Ent⁄wicklung des Trockengebietes am Nordrand Südamerikas seit dem Pleis⁄tozän', in *Die Erde,* 3–4, (Berlin, 1954); Hans Trojer, 'El tiempo reinante en Colombia', in *Boletín Técnico,* II: 13, 1–43, Federación Nacional de Cafeteros, (Chinchiná, 1954). A valuable source are the three volumes of the *Atlas de Economía Colombiana,* published by the Banco de la Re⁄pública, (Bogotá, 1959–62). An excellent popular introduction is Kathleen Romoli, *Colombia: Gateway to South America,* (New York, 1941); More recent is A. Curtis Wilgus (editor), *The Caribbean: Con⁄temporary Colombia,* (Gainesville, 1962).

CHAPTER III

6 On climatic changes see G. E. Maarleveld and Th. van der Hammen, 'The Correlation between Upper Pleistocene Pluvial and Glacial Stages', *GM,* 21, (1959), 40–45; Th. van der Hammen and E. González, 'Upper Pleistocene and Holocene Climate and Vegetation of the Sabana de Bogotá, Colombia, South America', *Leidse Geologische Mededelingen,* 25, (1960), 261–315; Th. van der Hammen and E. González, 'Holocene and Late Glacial Climate and Vegetation of Páramo de Palacio (Eastern Cordillera, Colombia, South America)', *GM,* 39:12, (1960), 737–745; Th. van der Hammen, 'The Quaternary Climatic Changes of Northern South America', *Annals of the New York Academy of Sciences,* 95, (1961), 676–683; Thomas van der Hammen, 'Palinología de la región de La⁄guna de los Bobos', *RACC,* XI: 44, (1962), 359–361; Th. van der Hammen and E. González, 'A Pollen Diagram from the Quaternary of the Sabana de Bogotá (Colombia) and its significance for the Geology of the Northern Andes', *GM,* 43, (1964), 113–117; E. González and

Th. van der Hammen, 'Late Quaternary Glacial and Vegetational Sequence in Valle de Lagunillas, Sierra Nevada del Cocuy', *Leidse Geologische Mededelingen* (in press); H.C.Raasveldt, 'Las glaciaciones de la
Sierra Nevada de Santa Marta', *RAAC*, IX:38, (1957), 469–482; Herbert Wilhelmy, 'Eiszeit und Eiszeitklima in den feuchttropischen Anden',
in *Machatschek-Festschrift*, 281–310, (n.d.). On late Pleistocene fauna
see Jaime de Porta, 'La posición estratigráfica de la fauna de mamíferos
del Pleistoceno de la Sabana de Bogotá', *BG*, 7 (1961), 37–54; *id.*,
'Algunos problemas estratigráfico-faunísticos de los vertebrados en
Colombia (con una bibliografía comentada)', *BG*, 7 (1961), 83–104;
id., 'A propósito de E.(Amerhippus) curvidens en el Pleistoceno de
Colombia', *Geologia Colombiana*, 2 (Bogotá, 1962) 35–39. Drifts I–IV
in Fig. 4 (page 43) refer to glacial advances in the Sierra Nevada del
Cocuy, Eastern Cordillera, while the Bolívar and Mamancanaca Phases
are glacial advances in the Sierra Nevada of Santa Marta.

7 For a recent discussion of the Darien passage see S.K.Lothrop, 'Early
   Migrations to Central and South America: An Anthropological Prob-
   lem in the Light of Other Sciences', *Journal of the Royal Anthropological
   Institute*, 91:1 (London, 1961), 97–123.

8 On San Nicolás see G. and A.Reichel-Dolmatoff, 'Reconocimiento
   arqueológico de la hoya del rio Sinú', *RCA*, VI (1958), 31–149.

9 See also José de Recasens, 'Persistencia en la cultura Colima de una
   técnica paleolítica', *RIEN*, II: 1 (1945), 153–155; Emilio Robledo,
   'Migraciones oceánicas en el poblamiento de Colombia', *BIA*, I: 3
   (1955), 1–20.

10 For a recent résumé see Alex D.Krieger, 'Early Man in the New World',
    in Jesse D.Jennings and Edward Norbeck (editors), *Prehistoric Man in
    the New World*, 23–81, (Chicago, 1964).

CHAPTER IV

11 G.Reichel-Dolmatoff, 'Puerto Hormiga: Un complejo prehistórico

marginal en Colombia (Nota preliminar)', *RCA*, X (1961), 349–354.

12 G.Reichel-Dolmatoff, 'Conchales de la costa Caribe de Colombia', in *Actas del XXXI Congreso Internacional de Americanistas, São Paulo, 1954*, II (São Paulo, 1955), 619–626; *id.*, 'Excavaciones en los conchales de la Costa de Barlovento', *RCA*, IV (1955), 249–272.

13 The fibre-tempered pottery of the Zambrano region was first discovered in the early thirties by Gladys Ayer Nomland and a collection of sherds is in the Alfred L.Kroeber Museum of Anthropology, University of California, Berkeley. The collection, labelled C–113, is said to come from San Jacinto, a neighbouring municipality which, at that time, extended to the Magdalena river, just north of Zambrano. Our Buca-relia and Nomland's San Jacinto sites are probably the same. I owe a description of the Nomland collection to Dr John H.Rowe of Berkeley. For Isla de los Indios see G. and A.Reichel-Dolmatoff, 'Investigaciones arqueológicas en el Departamento del Magdalena: 1946–1950. Parte III: Arqueología del Bajo Magdalena', in *DE*, III; 4 (1953), 1–98.

CHAPTER V

14 David J. Rogers, 'Studies of Manihot esculenta Crantz and related species', *Bulletin of the Torrey Botanical Club*, 90:1 (New York, 1963), 43–54.

15 See Carlos Angulo Valdés, 'Evidence of the Barrancoid Series in North-ern Colombia', in A.Curtis Wilgus (editor), *The Caribbean: Contempo-rary Colombia*, (Gainesville, 1962), 35–46; *id.*, 'Evidencias de la Serie Barrancoide en el Norte de Colombia', *RCA*, XI (1962), 75–87; J.M. Cruxent and Irving Rouse, *An Archaeological Chronology of Venezuela*, 2 vol., Pan American Union, (Washington, 1958–59).

16 G.Reichel-Dolmatoff, 'The Formative Stage: An Appraisal from the Colombian Perspective', *Actas del XXXIII Congreso Internacional de Ame-ricanistas, San José, 1958*, (San José, 1959), II, 152–164.

17 G. and A.Reichel-Dolmatoff, 'Momil, Excavaciones en el Sinú', *RCA*,

V (1956), 111–333; *id.*, 'Momil: A Formative Sequence from the Sinú Valley, Colombia', *AA*, 22:3 (1957), 226–234.

18 Carl O. Sauer, 'Age and Area of American Cultivated Plants', *Actas del XXXIII Congreso Internacional de Americanistas, San José, 1958,* (San José, 1959), I, 215–229. On maize see L. M. Roberts and others, 'Razas de maíz en Colombia', *Boletín Técnico,* No. 2, Ministerio de Agricultura, (Bogotá, 1957).

19 G. Reichel-Dolmatoff, 'Anthropomorphic Figurines from Colombia: Their Magic and Art', in *Essays in Pre-Columbian Art and Archaeology,* (Samuel K. Lothrop, editor), (Cambridge, 1961), 229–241.

CHAPTER VI

20 G. Reichel-Dolmatoff, 'The Agricultural Basis of the Sub-Andean Chiefdoms of Colombia', in J. Wilbert (editor), *The Evolution of Horti-cultural Systems in Native America: Causes and Consequences,* (Caracas, 1961), 83–100.

21 There exists a voluminous bibliography on San Agustín; some of the more important publications are: K. Th. Preuss, *Monumentale vorgeschicht-liche Kunst: Ausgrabungen im Quellgebiet des Magdalena in Kolumbien und ihre Ausstrahlungen in Amerika,* (Göttingen, 1929); José Pérez de Barradas, *Arqueología Agustiniana,* (Bogotá, 1943); Henri Lehmann, 'Arqueología de Moscopán', *RIEN,* II:2 (1944), 657–670; Luis Duque Gómez, Los últimos hallazgos arqueológicos en San Agustín', *RI,* 96 (1947), 387–418; *id., San Agustín: Reseña Arqueológica,* (Bogotá, 1963). Some other publications are: Federico Lunardi, *El Macizo Colombiano en la prehistoria de Sur América,* (Rio de Janeiro, 1934); *id., La vida en las tumbas,* (Rio de Janeiro, 1935).

22 Juan de Santa Gertrudis, *Maravillas de la Naturaleza,* 2 vol., Biblioteca de la Presidencia de Colombia, No. 28–29 (Bogotá, 1956).

23 Luis Duque Gómez, *San Agustín: Reseña Arqueológica,* (Bogotá, 1963), 103–108.

24 Juan Friede, 'Reseña etnográfica de los Macaguajes de San Joaquín sobre el Putumayo', *BA*, I:6 (1945), 553–598.

25 On Tierradentro see G. Bürg, 'Beitrag zur Ethnographie Südkolumbiens auf Grund eigener Forschungen', *Ibero-Amerikanisches Archiv*, XI:3, (Berlin-Bonn, 1937), 333–375; José Pérez de Barradas, *Arqueología y antropología precolombinas de Tierradentro,* (Bogotá, 1937); Gregorio Hernández de Alba, 'Investigaciones arqueológicas en Tierradentro', *RI*, II:9–10 (1938); *id.,* 'The Archaeology of San Agustin and Tierradentro', Handbook of South American Indians, *Bureau of American Ethnology, Bulletin* 143, II (Washington, 1946), 851–859; Eliécer Silva Celis, 'La arqueología de Tierradentro', *RIEN*, I:1 (1943), 117–130; *id.,* I:II (1944), 521–589; Horst Nachtigall, *Tierradentro: Archäologie und Ethnographie einer kolumbianischen Landschaft,* (Zurich, 1955).

26 For a discussion of the chronological relationships between San Agustín and Tierradentro see Helmut Ziegert, 'Zur Chronologie der Tierradentro- und San-Agustin-Kultur (Kolumbien)', *ZE,* 87 (Brunswick, 1962), 51–55, and Horst Nachtigall, under the same title *ZE,* 89 (Brunswick, 1964), 78–81.

27 On Calima see Henry Wassén, 'An Archaeological Study in the Western Colombian Cordillera', *ES, 2* (Göteborg, 1936); Roberto Pineda G., 'Material arqueológico de la zona Calima', *BA,* I:6 (1945), 491–518; José Pérez de Barradas, *Orfebrería prehispánica de Colombia: Estilo Calima,* 2 vol., (Madrid, 1954); Warwick Bray, 'Investigaciones arqueológicas en el Valle del Calima', *RCA,* XI (1962), 321–328.

28 See Ernesto Restrepo Tirado, *Ensayo etnográfico y arqueológico de la provincia de los Quimbayas en el Nuevo Reino de Granada,* (Seville, 1929); Juan Friede, *Los Quimbayas bajo la dominación española,* (Bogotá, 1963); Luis Duque Gómez, 'Los Quimbayas', in *Historia de Pereira,* (Bogotá, 1963), 3–174; *id.,* 'Mutilaciones dentarias prehispánicas en Colombia', in *A Pedro Bosch Gimpera en el septuagésimo aniversario de su nacimiento,* (Mexico, 1963), 157–160.

29 From the voluminous literature on aboriginal gold-work in Colombia, the following publications are of major importance: Paul Bergsøe, 'The Metallurgy and Technology of Gold and Platinum among the Pre Columbian Indians', *Ingeniørvidenskabelige Skrifter*, No. a 44, (Copenhagen, 1937); P.Rivet et H.Arsandaux, 'La métallurgie en Amérique précolombienne', Université de Paris, *Travaux et Mémoires de l'Institut d'Ethnologie, XXXIX* (Paris, 1946); G.Reichel-Dolmatoff, 'Notas sobre la metalurgia prehistórica en el Litoral Caribe de Colombia', in *Homenaje al Profesor Paul Rivet*, Academia Colombiana de Historia, (Bogotá, 1953), 79–94; Luis Duque Gómez, 'Notas históricas sobre la orfebrería indígena de Colombia', *op.cit.*, 271–335; Dudley T.Easby, *Orfebrería y orfebres precolombinos*, Instituto de Arte Americano, (Buenos Aires, 1956); José Pérez de Barradas, *Orfebrería Prehispánica de Colombia: Estilo Calima*, 2 vol., (Madrid, 1954); *id., Orfebrería Prehispánica de Colombia: Estilos Tolima y Muisca*, 2 vol., (Madrid, 1958); A.M.Barriga Villalba, 'Orfebrería Chibcha y su definición científica', *RACC*, XI: 43 (Bogotá, 199–211.

30 See John H.Rowe, 'The Potter's Art of Atacames', *Archaeology*, 2:1 (New York, 1949), 31–34; Julio César Cubillos, *Tumaco: Notas arqueológicas*, (Bogotá, 1955); Horst Nachtigall, 'Tumaco: Ein Fundort der Esmeraldas-Kultur in Kolumbien', *Baessler-Archiv*, Neue Folge, III (Berlin, 1955). 97–121.

31 The origin of these double-spouted vessels is unknown. The main centre of distribution in the Americas are the western sections of Colombia, Ecuador, and Peru.

32 For relationships between Mesoamerica, and Peru and Ecuador, see among others, Muriel Noe Porter, *Tlatilco and the Pre-Classic Cultures of the New World*, Viking Fund Publications in Anthropology, No. 19, (New York, 1953); Gordon R.Willey, 'The Interrelated Rise of the Native Cultures of Middle and South America', in *New Interpretations of Aboriginal American Culture History*, 75th Anniversary Volume of the

Anthropological Society of Washington, (Washington, 1955), 28-45; Michael D. Coe, 'Archaeological Linkages with North and South America at La Victoria, Guatemala', *American Anthropologist*, 62:3 (Menasha, 1960), 363-393; Emilio Estrada and Clifford Evans, 'Cultural Development in Ecuador', in *Aboriginal Cultural Developments in Latin America: An Interpretative Review*, (Betty J. Meggers and Clifford Evans, editors), Smithsonian Institution, (Washington, 1963), 77-88; Alfred Kidder II, 'South American High Cultures', in *Prehistoric Man in the New World*, (Jesse D. Jennings and Edward Norbeck, editors), (Chicago, 1964), 451-486; Furst, P. T., 'Radiocarbon Dates from a Tomb in Mexico', *Science*, Vol. 147, No. 3658, pp. 612-613, (Washington, 1965).

CHAPTER VII

33   G. and A. Reichel-Dolmatoff, 'Investigaciones arqueológicas en el Departamento del Magdalena: 1946-50, Parte I: Arqueología del río Ranchería', *BA*, III:1-6 (Bogotá, 1951), 1-334.

34   J. M. Cruxent and Irving Rouse, *op. cit.*

35   G. and A. Reichel-Dolmatoff, 'Investigaciones arqueológicas en el Departamento del Magdalena: 1946-50, Parte II: Arqueología de río Cesar', *BA*, (Bogotá, 1951).

36   Carlos Angulo Valdés, 'Arqueología de Tubará', *DE*, II:3 (Barranquilla, 1951), 7-52.

37   G. and A. Reichel-Dolmatoff, 'Reconocimiento arqueológico en la hoya del río Sinú', *RCA*, VI (Bogotá, 1958), 31-149.

38   Alicia Dussan de Reichel, 'Crespo: Un nuevo complejo arqueológico del Norte de Colombia', *RCA*, III (Bogotá, 1954), 173-188.

39   G. and A. Reichel-Dolmatoff, 'Investigaciones arqueológicas en la Costa Pacífica de Colombia, II: Una secuencia cultural del bajo río San Juan', *RCA*, XI (Bogotá, 1962), 11-62.

40   S. Linné, *Darien in the Past: The Archaeology of Eastern Panama and North-*

Western Colombia, (Göteborg, 1929), *cf.* 176–202; G. and A. Reichel-Dolmatoff, 'Investigaciones arqueológicas en la Costa Pacífica de Colombia, I: El sitio de Cupica', *RCA*, X (Bogotá, 1961), 239–317; *id.,* 'Una nueva fecha de Carbono-14 de Colombia', *op.cit.,* XI (Bogotá, 1962). 331–332.

41 Henri Lehmann, 'Archéologie du sud-ouest colombien', *Journal de la Société des Américanistes,* N.S., XLII (Paris, 1953), 199–270.

42 Henri Lehmann, *op.cit.*

43 On this region see also Henri Lehmann, 'Notas arqueológicas sobre el Cauca', *Revista de la Universidad del Cauca,* 1 (Popayán, 1943), 196–201.

44 James A. Ford, *Excavations in the Vicinity of Cali,* Yale University Publications in Anthropology, No. 31, (New Haven, 1944).

45 Henry Wassén, *op.cit.*

46 There exist several site reports on excavations and surveys in this area, but detailed pottery descriptions are rare and no local sequences have been established. See Graciliano Arcila Vélez, 'Arqueología de Mutatá', *BIA*, I:1 (Medellín, 1953), 7–50; *id.,* 'Estudio preliminar de la cultura rupestre en Antioquia: Támesis', *op.cit.,* II:5 (1956), 5–22; *id.* 'Investigaciones antropológicas en el Carmen de Atrato, Departamento del Chocó', *op.cit.,* II:7 (1960), 3–38; Ida Cerezo Lopez, 'Breve estudio de algunas pintaderas-rodillos del Departamento de Antioquia, Colombia', *op.cit.,* (1962), 104–122. On the sixteenth-century ethnography of the Cauca Chiefdoms see Hermann Trimborn, *Vergessene Königreiche: Studien zur Völkerkunde und Altertumskunde Nordwest-Kolumbiens,* (Brunswick, n.d.).

47 On urn-burials see G. and A. Reichel-Dolmatoff, 'Las urnas funerarias en la cuenca del río Magdalena', *RIEN,* I:1 (Bogotá, 1943), 209–281; Among site reports see Julio César Cubillos, 'Arqueología de Rioblanco', *BA,* II:6 (Bogotá, 1945), 519–530; Julio César Cubillos and Victor E. Bedoya, 'Arqueología de las riberas del río Magdalena, Espinal, Tolima', *RCA,* II (Bogotá, 1954), 117–144.

48 Paul Rivet, 'La influencia karib en Colombia', *RIEN,* I: 1 (Bogotá, 1943), 55–87.

49 Gonzalo Fernández de Oviedo y Valdés, *Historia general y natural de las Indias, islas y tierra-firme del mar Océano,* (Madrid, 1851–55), II, 449.

50 Pedro Aguado, *Recopilación Historial,* (Bogotá, 1956–57), I, 601–602.

51 On pictographs and petroglyphs see José Pérez de Barradas, *El arte rupestre en Colombia,* Consejo Superior de Investigaciones Científicas, Instituto Bernardino de Sahagún, Serie A, No. 1, (Madrid, 1941); Theodor Koch-Grünberg, *Südamerikanische Felszeichnungen,* (Berlin, 1907).

CHAPTER VIII

52 On the Tairona see Gustaf Bolinder, 'Urn-burial in full-size mortuary urns in Sierra Nevada de Santa Marta, Colombia', *Ethnos,* 1 (Stockholm, 1942), 10–19; J. Alden Mason, *Archaeology of Santa Marta, Colombia. The Tairona Culture,* Field Museum of Natural History, Anthropological Series, XX: 1–2–3 (Chicago, 1931, 1936, 1939); Gregory Mason, *South of Yesterday,* (New York, 1940); G. Reichel-Dolmatoff, *Datos histórico-culturales sobre las tribus de la antigua Gobernación de Santa Marta,* (Bogotá, 1951); G. and A. Reichel-Dolmatoff, 'Investigaciones arqueológicas en la Sierra Nevada de Santa Marta', *RCA,* II (Bogotá, 1954), 147–206; III (Bogotá, 1954), 141–170; IV (Bogotá, 1955), 191–245; *id.,* 'La Mesa: Un complejo arqueológico de la Sierra Nevada de Santa Marta', *RCA,* VIII (Bogotá, 1959), 161–213.

53 Juan de Castellanos, *Elegías de varones ilustres,* (Madrid, 1847), cf. 261, 264.

54 Pedro Simón, *Noticias historiales de las conquistas de Tierra Firme en las Indias Occidentales,* (Bogotá, 1882–92), cf. V, 191.

55 Oviedo, *op.cit.*

56 On the modern Indians of the Sierra Nevada see Konrad Theodor Preuss, *Forschungsreise zu den Kágaba,* (Vienna, 1926); G. Reichel-Dolmatoff, *Los Kogi: Una tribu indígena de la Sierra Nevada de Santa Marta, Colombia,* 2 vol.,

(Bogotá, 1950–51); *id.,* 'Contactos y cambios culturales en la Sierra Nevada de Santa Marta', *RCA,* 1, (Bogotá, 1953), 17–122.

57 Ernesto Restrepo Tirado, 'Cómo se pacificaba a los indios', *Boletín de Historia y Antigüedades,* XXIV:278 (Bogotá, 1937), 739–743.

58 On Chibcha culture see Sylvia M. Broadbent, *Los Chibchas: organización socio-política,* Serie Latinoamericana, No. 5, Facultad de Sociología, Universidad Nacional, (Bogotá, 1964); Gregorio Hernández de Alba, 'Descubrimientos arqueológicos en tierras de los Chibchas: Laguna de Fúquene', *Boletín del Museo Arqueológico de Colombia,* II:1, 23–30, (Bogotá, 1944); Alfred L. Kroeber, 'The Chibcha', Handbook of South American Indians, *Bureau of American Ethnology, Bulletin* 143, (Washington, 1946), II, 887–909; José Pérez de Barradas, *Los Muiscas antes de la Conquista,* 2 vol., Consejo Superior de Investigaciones Científicas, Instituto Bernardino de Sahagún, (Madrid, 1950–51); Vicente Restrepo, *Los Chibchas antes de la conquista española,* (Bogotá, 1895); *id., Atlas Arqueológico,* (Paris, 1895); Eliécer Silva Celis, 'Sobre antropología Chibcha', *BA,* II:6 (Bogotá, 1945), 531–551; *id.,* 'Contribución al conocimiento de la civilización Lache', *BA,* II:5 (Bogotá, 1945), 371–424.

59 Emil W. Haury and Julio César Cubillos, 'Investigaciones arqueológicas en la Sabana de Bogotá, Colombia (Cultura Chibcha)' *University of Arizona, Bulletin* XXIV:2 (Tucson, 1953).

60 Gregorio Hernández de Alba, 'El Templo del Sol de Goronchacha', *RI,* II:7 (Bogotá, 1937), 10–18.

61 Eliécer Silva Celis, 'Investigaciones arqueológicas en Sogamoso', *BA,* I:1 (Bogotá, 1945), 36–48; I:2 (Bogotá, 1945) 93–112; I:4 (Bogotá, 1945), 283–297; I:6 (Bogotá, 1945), 467–490.

62 Federico Lunardi (1935), *op.cit.;* cf. figs. 114–115.

63 H. C. Raasveldt, *Los enigmas de la Laguna de Guatavita,* Instituto Geológico Nacional, (Bogotá, 1954).

Bibliography

General Works of Reference

ANGULO VALDES, CARLOS, 'Cultural Development in Colombia', in *Aboriginal Cultural Development in Latin America: An interpretative Review*, (Betty J. Meggers and Clifford Evans, editors), 55–56, Smithsonian Institution, (Washington, 1963).

BENNET, WENDELL C., *Archaeological Regions of Colombia: A Ceramic Survey*, Yale University Publications in Anthropology, No. 30, (New Haven, 1944).

—, 'The Archaeology of Colombia', Handbook of South American Indians, Vol. 2, 823–850, *Bureau of American Ethnology, Bulletin* 143, (Washington, 1946).

BENNETT, WENDELL C. and JUNIUS B. BIRD, *Andean Culture History* American Museum of Natural History, Handbook Series No. 15, (New York, 1949).

DUQUE GOMEZ, LUIS, *Colombia: Monumentos Históricos y Arqueológicos*, 2 vol., Instituto Panamericano de Geografía e Historia; Comisión de Historia, (Mexico, 1955).

JOYCE, T. A., *South American Archaeology*, (London, 1912).

NACHTIGALL, HORST, *Indianerkunst der Nord-Anden: Beiträge zu ihrer Typologie*, (Berlin, 1961).

—, *Alt-Kolumbien: Vorgeschichtliche Indianerkulturen*, (Berlin, 1961).

PEREZ DE BARRADAS, JOSE, *Colombia de Norte a Sur*, 2 vol., Ministerio de Asuntos Exteriores, (Madrid, 1943).

—, *El arte rupestre en Colombia*, Consejo Superior de Investigaciones Científicas, Instituto Bernardino de Sahagún, Serie A. No. 1, (Madrid, 1941).

REICHEL-DOLMATOFF, G., 'A Preliminary Study of Space and Time

Perspective in Northern Colombia', American Antiquity, Vol. 19, 352–366, (Salt Lake City, 1954).

—, 'Recientes investigaciones arqueológicas en el Norte de Colombia', in: Miscellanea Paul Rivet octogenario dicata, 2 vol., 471–485, Universidad Nacional Autónoma de México, (Mexico, 1958).

Sources of Illustrations

The following photographs were taken at the Museo Nacional, with the kind permission of the Instituto Colombiano de Antropología: 12, 13, 15–17, 19–21, 23, 27, 30, 41, 55, 56, 58–62. Grateful acknowledgement is made to the following for permission to publish their photographs: Instituto Colombiano de Antropología, 7, 8, 10, 11; Museo del Oro, 14, 18, 24–26, 31, 32, 63; Dr Yves Pret, Cali, 22; Professor Vidal Antonio Rozo, Bogotá, 9; Dr Fred Medem, Cartagena, 64, 65; Dr John H. Rowe, University of California, Berkeley, 2, 3.

The line drawings were made by Mrs Pauline Bright of Bogotá; Fig. 10a, b, c, was redrawn from Emilio Robledo (1955); 28, 43 from I. Cerezo Lopez (1962); 36 from Henry Wassén (1936); 63 was drawn by Mr Alec Bright. Fig. 2 is based on a diagram in the Atlas de Economía Colombiana.

THE PLATES

1

2

3

4

5

6

8

9

10

11

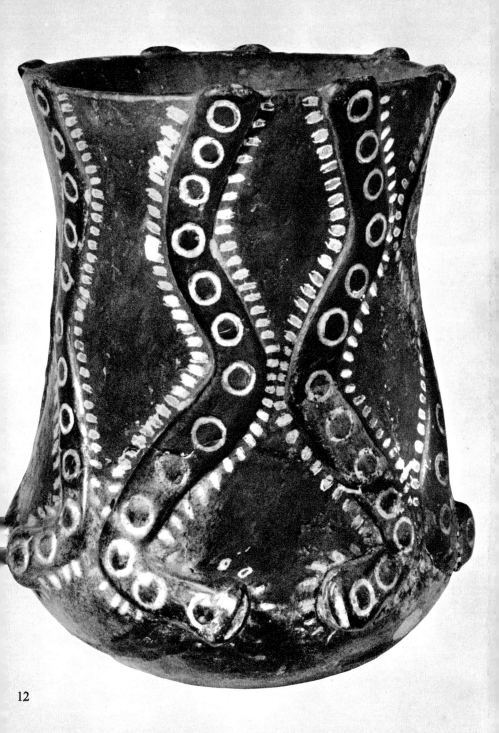

13

14

15

17

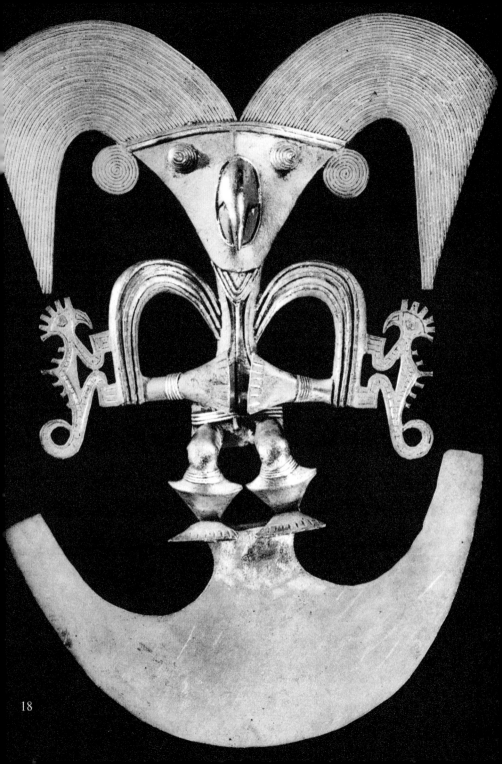

19

20

21

22

23

24

25

26

27

28

29

30

32

33

34

35

36

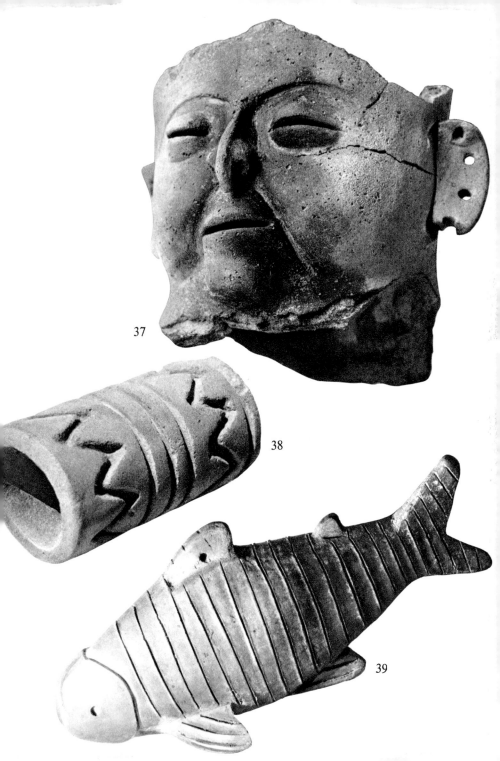

37

38

39

40

41

42

43

44

45

46

47

48

49

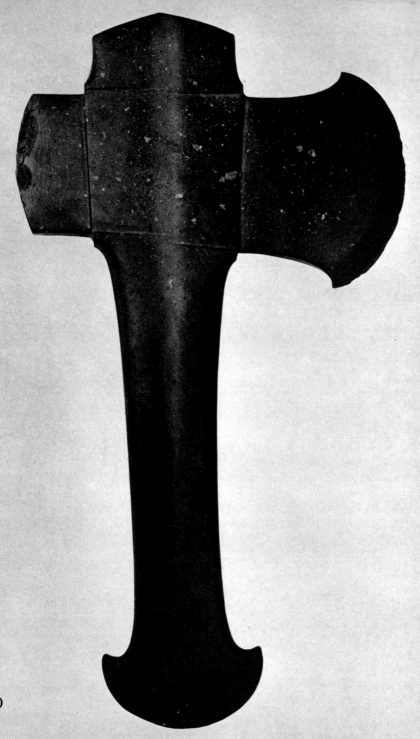

51

52

53

54

55

56

57

58

59

60

61

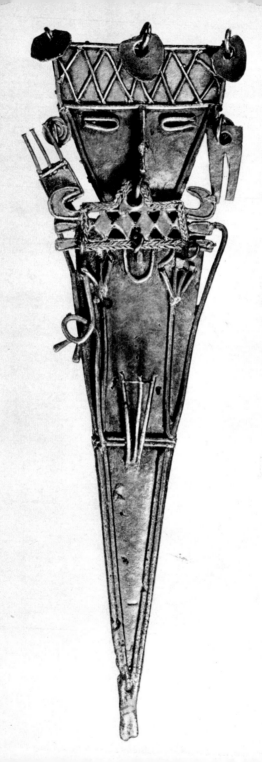

64

65

Notes on the Plates

1   Puerto Hormiga shell-mound, Caribbean lowlands. A human face, modelled and incised on the flat, out-flaring rim of a large bowl. This is one of the oldest anthropomorphic representations in aboriginal American art. About 3000 BC.

2, 3   Bucarelia, near Zambrano; lower Magdalena river. Fragments of fibre-tempered pottery of Puerto Hormiga type. These sherds form part of the Nomland Collection in the Robert H. Lowie Museum of Anthropology, University of California, Berkeley.

4   Puerto Hormiga shell-mound, Carribbean lowlands. These zoomorphic modellings on the rim of large bowls are very characteristic of this stage. About 3000 BC.

5   Momil, Sinú river. Solid clay figurine from Period I. This is one of the very few whole specimens; all others are fragmentary, having been broken, probably intentionally after having fulfilled a ritual function. Many hundreds of these figurines are found in the midden refuse. Some of them show traces of paint.

6   Ciénaga de Oro, Sinú river. Head of a hollow clay figurine. This site is related to the Momil complex, but the figurines are more elaborate and are decorated with incised designs.

7   Moscopán, near Popayán, upper Cauca valley. This statue of late San Agustín type, discovered by Henri Lehmann in 1943, is 1.65 m. high. Originally it was painted red. Compared with other San Agustín statues it is unique for its realism. It stands today in the main court of the Universidad del Cauca, Popayán.

8 San Agustín, Eastern Mound of Mesita A. Statue of a warrior, armed with a club and carrying an *alter ego* representation. Height, 2 m.

9 San Agustín. This statue, discovered in 1964, is the only one which represents the body in movement. The V-shaped chest-marking is also a unique feature.

10 San Agustín, El Tablón site. A statue ostensibly representing a woman, adorned with a nose-ring, an elaborate necklace, bracelets and multiple ear-plugs. Height, 2.83 m.

11 San Agustín, North Mound of Mesita B. This statue combines human with feline features. A trophy skull is suspended from the neck. Height, 2.27 m.

12 Tierradentro. A large vessel decorated with snake-like relief bands. The incisions are filled with a white pigment.

13 'Quimbaya'. A double-spouted vessel with a loop handle. The part above the shoulder is decorated with painted designs. For another vessel of similar type see Plate 23.

14 'Quimbaya' style; from Pajarito, district of Antioquia. A golden flask weighing 777.70 grams and measuring 23.3 cm.

15 'Quimbaya' area; probably from the northern part of the Valle district. Slab-shaped figurine of clay. The hollow interior contains a pebble which produces a rattling noise when the object is shaken.

16 'Quimbaya' area; Central Cordillera. An anthropomorphic vessel representing a person sitting cross-legged.

17 'Quimbaya' area. A square pottery container with champ-levé decoration. The design probably represents a pattern woven in basketry. Height,
14 cm.

18 Popayán area, Hacienda La Marquesa. A gold figurine wearing an elaborate head-dress. The legs show ligatures below the knees and above the
ankles, deforming the calves.

19 Nariño area. A deep dish decorated with spiral elements painted in red
on a white base.

20 Nariño area. This conical cup is decorated with negative paint in white
and black on a red base. It is closely related to 'Quimbaya' ceramics.
Height, 10 cm.

21 Calima area, village of El Darien. Anthropomorphic vessel representing
a sitting woman with braided hair and a necklace with a pendant. The
shoulders are decorated with stamped circles. The cylindrical container
on the back of the figurine is fragmented, in this case.

22 Calima area. Anthropomorphic vessel with incised decoration.

23 Calima area. Double-spouted vessel with incised decoration. This characteristic form appears about 500 BC in the Tumaco area. See also Plate 13.

24 Calima area, village of Restrepo. This golden diadem is a very elaborate
piece of workmanship. The human mask in the centre wears an H-shaped
nose ornament which, in its turn, represents a face with feline features.
A third face is represented on a band which projects vertically from the
upper part. Spool-shaped ear-rings and tubular pendants are added in
profusion. Weight, 174.4 g.; height, 28.3 cm.

25 Calima area, village of Restrepo. Spool-shaped ear ornament of gold. Diameter, 8.8 cm,; weight, 86.15 g.

26 Calima area, village of Restrepo. Crescent-shaped nose ornament with tubular bangles and a number of circular convex disks which are suspended in the perforations adorning the upper part. Weight, 48.25 g.; width, 18 cm.

27 Tumaco area; La Playa, Mira river. Large head of a hollow clay figurine of excellent workmanship. The strong features are reminiscent of Peruvian ceramics.

28 Tumaco area; Mira river. A fragment of a hollow figurine representing a sitting person. Height, 17 cm.

29 Tumaco area; a mould-made figurine representing a person whose face looks out through the wide-open beak of a monstrous bird-mask. Height, 9 cm.

30 Tumaco area. This decapitated figurine has its head placed inside its body. Similar figurines have been found at Teotihuacán, in Mexico.

31 Darien style. A highly abstract figurine of gold. Weight, 293 g.; height, 17 cm.

32 Tolima style. This gold pendant represents a fantastic winged being, very typical of this stylistic area. Weight, 187.4 g.; height, 19.2 cm.

33 Middle Magdalena valley; Río de la Miel. Burial urn with incised and modelled decoration. A figurine, adorned with small perforated shell disks, sits on the lid. The calves of the legs are deformed by ligatures. The urn contained burned human bones. Height, 57 cm.

34 Lower Magdalena valley; region of Tamalameque. An unopened shaft grave. These graves are about 2 m. deep and the side chambers contain urns of the type shown on Plates 35, 36.

35, 36 Lower Magdalena valley; region of Tamalameque. Cylindrical burial urns with anthropomorphic covers. Both types occur in the same grave.

37 Lower Magdalena valley; Zambrano area. Anthropomorphic vessel (fragment) with realistic features.

38 Lower Magdalena valley, Zambrano area. A tubular clay stamp with simple incised decoration.

39 Lower Magdalena valley; Zambrano area. A fish effigy of clay. The dorsal fin has a suspension hole.

40 Sinú area, Betancí site. A globular vessel decorated with painted designs.

41 San Jorge area. Realistic figurine showing a man sitting on a four-legged stool and holding a staff, the upper end of which is broken off. Probably the lid of a burial urn.

42 Sinú area, Betancí site. Tall pedestal cup (fragmented) with female figurines surrounding the base.

43 Sinú area, Betancí site. Black-ware vessel with excised decoration.

44 Cartagena area, Crespo site. A ring-base cup with incised decoration.

45 Lower Magdalena valley; Zambrano area. A globular vessel with annular base, short neck, and out-flaring rim.

46 Lower Magdalena valley; Zambrano area. A so-called shoe-shaped vessel. Often these vessels have a handle and a strong conical lateral projection.

47 Cartagena area, Crespo site. A globular vessel with restricted orifice.

48 Upper Córdoba river, Sierra Nevada of Santa Marta; Tairona area. A ceremonial structure with stepped platforms and staircases.

49 Pueblito, Sierra Nevada of Santa Marta; Tairona area. Stone-built house foundations. Underneath some of the horizontal slabs small caches of ceremonial objects are often found.

50 Pueblito, Sierra Nevada of Santa Marta; Tairona area. A monolithic ceremonial axe of dark-green andesite. Length, 22 cm.

51 Bonda, Sierra Nevada of Santa Marta; Tairona area. Fragment of a bio-morphic ocarina. The dragon-like figure wears a feather head-dress and shows snake-like fangs and a protruding tongue.

52 Pueblito, Sierra Nevada of Santa Marta; Tairona area. A ceremonial vessel with snake-shaped supports.

53 Jirocasaca, Sierra Nevada of Santa Marta; Tairona area. Figurine of gild-ed copper. A human body is combined with a feline head adorned with a semicircular head-dress. At both sides of the body there are snake heads in wire-work. The lower half consists of a flat leaf-shaped blade.

54 Bonda, Sierra Nevada of Santa Marta; Tairona area. Figurine of gilded copper. Again a feline head is combined with a human body.

55,56 La Belleza; Chibcha area. Votive offerings of soft stone; hundreds of

these figurines were found in caves. Similar effigies of stone were found in
the lagoon of Fúquene.

57   Sibaté; Chibcha area. This mummy of an infant was found in a cave.
     From its neck was suspended a large *millefiori* bead.

58   Chibcha area. A hemispherical container with decorated rim and a bas-
     ket handle.

59   Chibcha area. This anthropomorphic vessel shows the shield-shaped face
     typical of Chibcha art.

60   Chibcha area. Pedestal bowls of this type are very common. The painted
     decoration sometimes includes stylized animal figures.

61   Chibcha area. Large vessel with painted decoration.

62   Chibcha area. Anthropomorphic vessel with bar-shaped nose plaque and
     'bandolier' ornaments. Some of these figurines carry cups, spear-throwers,
     or clubs.

63   Chibcha area. A typical wedge-shaped figurine of gold. The stylized
     features consist of wire-work on a thin plate.

64   Cerro de las Pinturas, Inírida river; Amazon area. Many rock shelters and
     cliffs are covered with pictographs showing mammals, fish, hands, or
     geometric elements. The central figure of this pictograph shows a jaguar.

65   La Pedrera, Caquetá river; Amazon area. Pecked or scratched petroglyphs
     are frequent in this and many other regions. In the Amazon area they are
     often found on boulders near rapids.

Index

Colombia

settlement patterns, 19, 52–53, 67, 80ff.,
    94, 100, 115, 117, 122, 123, 124, 125,
    128, 129, 130, 142–143, 161, 162
Sevilla river, 152
shell-mounds, 51ff., 58, 61, 66, 122
Sibaté, 164
Sierra Nevada of Santa Marta, 22, 24, 33,
    34, 95, 117, 120, 121, 122, 123, 137,
    142ff.
Silva Celis, Eliécer, 24
Sinú (area and culture), 19, 33, 48, 67ff.,
    122, 123, 125, 132
Socha Vieja, 163
social stratification, 75, 93–94, 110, 115,
    127, 160
Sogamoso, 161, 163
Spanish conquest, 18ff., 22, 86, 101–102,
    121–122, 128, 129, 134, 135, 136, 138,
    143, 144, 155–156, 158, 167
spindle whorls, 71, 72, 83, 105, 110, 115,
    123, 127, 131, 133, 134, 135, 138, 151,
    164, 166
stone sculpture, 20, 86ff., 96, 110, 154,
    166; statues, 89ff., 94, 95, 96, 163
statues, *see* stone sculpture, statues
stone tools, general, 40, 46ff., 48ff., 54,
    56–57, 58, 68, 71–72, 79, 83, 91, 93,
    124, 129, 131, 138, 152; choppers, 49,
    57; knives, 48ff., 93; grinding stones,
    metates, 71, 72, 73, 82, 85, 93, 117, 130,
    152, 161; *manos*, 61, 72, 73, 82, 85, 93,
    129, 130; scrapers, 48ff., 57, 71, 73,
    93, 130

Sub-Andean stage, 80ff., 115, 117, 123,
    125, 127, 136, 142, 144

Tacurumbí, 101
Tairona (area and culture), 19, 20, 21,
    121, 142ff.
Tamalameque, 138
terraces, 124, 158, 159
Tierra Alta, 125, 132
Tierradentro (area and culture), 21, 24,
    96ff., 101, 109, 110, 134
Tierra Bomba, Isla de, 59
tipití, 63
tolas, 111
tombs, *see* burials
Tolima (district), 46–47
trade, trade routes, 18, 38, 63, 64, 115, 117,
    123, 124, 143, 159
reasure-hunters, 18, 19, 23, 86, 99, 102,
    106, 126, 128, 134
Tubará, 124
Tumaco (area and culture), 84, 110,
    111ff., 132
tumbaga, 133, *see* metallurgy
Tunja, 158, 161
tunjos, 160

Urabá, Gulf of, 33, 37, 59, 68, 125, 128
Uribe Angel, Manuel, 21
Uricoechea, Ezequiel, 21
Utría, Bahía de, 49

Van der Hammen, Thomas, 41
Venezuela, 32, 34, 36, 37, 38, 46, 58, 64,
    66, 74, 120, 121, 139, 162